HOW I STOPPED HATING MY HUSBAND

Cindy Butler Carbone

HOW I STOPPED HATING MY HUSBAND

Cindy Butler Carbone

HOW I STOPPED HATING MY HUSBAND

Copyright © 2019 Cindy Butler Carbone

All rights reserved. No part of this book may be reproduced in any form or by any means—whether electronic, digital, mechanical, or otherwise—without permission in writing from the publisher, except by a reviewer, who may quote brief passages in a review.

Edited by Stephanie Siu
Photo credit: Tru Photography by Jaime Emfinger
Cover design by Ahmed Raza
Interior design by Roseanna White Designs

ISBN: 978-1-698-34441-6

I dedicate this book to my husband.

CONTENTS

"Vulnerability is the birthplace of innovation, creativity, and change."

– Brené Brown

PREFACE

Three years ago, I poured my heart into a blog post that would change my life. It was called, "How I Stopped Hating My Husband." It was like the story had been waiting to come out of me. The words gushed onto the page, and I knew I had to put it out in the world.

I shared a link to it on my Facebook page. Within hours I was getting messages, comments, texts, and calls from people I knew—and some I didn't. My mom, 2,000 miles away in Boston, called to say her friend's daughter-in-law had been talking about my article. People I went to school with couldn't believe what I had professed to the world. Folks I'd never met thanked me for making them feel less alone.

That blog post led to a health coaching business that

rejected conventional ideas for weight loss in favor of physical, mental, and emotional health. I invented a digital education tool teaching about food, health, and self-aware-ness, and began live group coaching in my home through plant-based food demonstrations.

When I started The Healthy Life Club, I envisioned a community based on accountability, empowerment, learning, authenticity, and courage. I wanted a space that brought people back to nature while they inspected their own ecologies. I also wanted to share all the tools I used to change my health and marriage with anyone brave enough to explore their inner life in the same way.

At the same time my fledgling business was taking off, I became known in the Texas suburb where I lived as the woman who wrote "that blog" about hating her spouse. I cannot tell you how many times I've introduced myself at an event and the other person has whispered, "I know you! You're the one who wrote that blog about your husband!"

A few months later, I wrote a sequel called "8 Things I Did to Fall Back in Love with My Husband." It did well, though it didn't have the life-changing effect of the origi-nal. Life carried on after that. Almost two years later, my coaching business was flourishing. Though I still fielded the occasional random message from readers, those posts felt way behind me.

All of a sudden, the trickle became a fountain again. I found myself getting more emails than ever, many of them from men. One guy from Australia was devastated that his wife wanted to separate. Another from San Francisco asked if I could console him over the phone.

I did my best to help, but these limited encounters never felt like enough. I was a beacon of hope to thousands of strangers. Women wanted to know how to return to their husbands. Husbands wanted to know if they could be loved again. Everyone wanted to know if it was possible to fall back in love.

I realized how misled many of us are about attachment. The idea of "falling" in or out or back into love was so passive and ineffective. It assumed a lack of power and control over our ability to love. This does a disservice to our relationships, which require time, attention, and intention to flourish. We have to tend to our mutual bonds. Connection is our healthiest, most natural state. Yet we value and invest in everything but that.

I read story after story of desperation and sadness, answering their questions the best I could via email. Yet I could never say everything I wanted to say. These people were watching their lives unravel—a feeling I knew well. I longed to give them more.

Then the social media expert I hired told me that hundreds of people were landing organically on my blog, not for food or health advice, but to read those two blogs about hating my husband and falling back in love with him again. I was dumbfounded that so many people were stumbling onto my story simply through their own desperate research. It was clear the problem was common, but my outcome was not.

For years, I'd wanted to write a book sharing everything I'd learned about personal transformation. It wasn't until I saw my website traffic that I knew where to start. It was a problem that thousands of people had, but no one dared discuss. A secret whispered in the ears of confidantes or relegated to late-night Google searches when you felt like you had nowhere else to turn.

They say you should write a book that would have helped *you*. Through my journey, I learned that the only way a relationship changes and becomes the best version of itself is when both parties become the best versions of themselves. The 10-step blueprint I outline here encompasses growth with our partner, but also within ourselves.

This book is part self-help and part memoir. I intentionally took an approach that is more personal than prescriptive. As a health coach, I steer clients away from solutions that mask symptoms rather than fix the underlying issue. That's because true change comes from a willingness to challenge ourselves. It's born from the emotional exercises that bring us to our knuckles and knees. In the language of nature, no flowers can bloom until you dig down in the dirt and heal your roots.

I intentionally kept this book brief. As an avid reader, I cherish books that challenge my thinking and experience in just one day. I also remember what it felt like in your shoes. At the lowest point in my marriage, I was desperate to find an answer—and fast. True healing takes time, but my hope is to inspire you to keep trying. I wanted to offer more of what people needed from my blog posts: reassurance that all is not lost, and the understanding that you are not alone.

Maybe you picked up this book because you were intrigued by the title but feel embarrassed to let anybody see you reading it. Perhaps you're worried it will spook your husband, who doesn't know how you feel. Just remember this is also an autobiography. You are allowed to be interested in my story whether you are happily single, love your spouse to death, have hated him for a decade, or if he/she just annoys the crap out of you once in a while.

I want to thank everyone who has supported me in writing this book. I want to thank my husband, Mario, especially. Without him, my internal makeover and our marital fulfillment would not be possible. When the going got tough, he took my hand and led us straight into the pain. I truly believe that's why we were able to rekindle our love. Together we chose to bare all, let go, stand up and fight like our life depended on it—because it did. This mutual effort saved our marriage, and we hope that it can save yours too.

INTRODUCTION

Whanes you don't love your spouse, that feeling of emptiness is invisible to the world but manifests itself in other ways. For years, I was physically present but emotionally disconnected. While I kept the outward appearance of a loving family, I seethed alone in my suffering. Yet I had no idea of the damage I was inflicting on my husband or our children until those wounds began to heal and it created a different energy within our home.

Looking back, I was so far gone that it is nothing short of remarkable that I was able to come back. The journey didn't happen to me. I made it happen.

The title of this book is "How I Stopped Hating My Husband," but I will tell you off the bat that you can't stop hating someone. Think about it. How does one "not" hate? What thoughts, emotions and behaviors amount to *not* hating? How can you engage in the negation of an experience?

It's absurd. Yet that is the approach many of us take with our physical and emotional health. We try to *not* eat junk, instead of balancing our diet with healthier foods. We try to *not* be negative, instead of focusing on everything that's good. We try to *not* be stressed, instead of engaging in thoughts and behaviors that foster calm. We spend so much time focusing on what *not* to do that everything starts to feel like a sacrifice.

Dan Millman famously wrote, "The secret of change is to focus all of your energy not on fighting the old, but on building the new." This book is about starting fresh. The principles here don't just apply to marriage, either. You can use these steps to affect anything in your life, because ultimately this book is about transforming yourself.

You may have come here with your own story of pain, resentment, blame, or disgust. Some of you may desperately want to save your marriage, while others have no desire to love their spouse again. All of that is you avoiding what's necessary for liberation. We often fool ourselves into thinking we do not have the power to change, which makes everything seem more complicated. Truth is simple. It's the lies we tell ourselves that make things appear difficult.

I want to help you understand how you got here, so you can begin to separate from that negative emotional state. Whether you ultimately stay or go, you need to be in the best frame of mind to make that decision. This will minimize the drama and hardship that will arise no matter which path you choose. Choices laced with toxicity are poison to all involved.

Nowhere in this book will you find excuses for what happened in my marriage. When we get defensive about the roles we played, we are resisting something we need to change within ourselves. The more we weaponize blame, the more we fight our own growth. Freedom comes from surrendering to our own evolution. This means holding ourselves accountable as creators of our own reality.

Many of us willfully take the passenger seat in our own lives. We sit there with our hands in the air as if to say, "It's not my fault, I'm not driving!" Over time, the front row becomes so crowded with other people and circumstances we have permitted to take the wheel that we fall further and further into powerlessness. A passive observer in our own lives, we become anxious and afraid.

For ten years, I resisted the call to grow as a person. I let my situation harden me instead. My mind was a prison, so my life became one. Think about that and repeat it to yourself. When your brain is trapped in an endless loop of the same ideas, emotions, and experiences, it's closed off to anything else. It simply perpetuates the same experience you've had day after day. My mind was like a broken record, stuck on the same tune. What I allowed myself to think, believe and consume became my habitual emotional state.

Once I assumed power over my mind, I could remove the thoughts and beliefs that had kept me unhappy and powerless. I had to remove everything else from the driver's seat and retake the wheel. The difference was remarkable. When I was less overwhelmed and could see my situation clearly, I realized I wanted to love my husband again. I wanted my marriage to work. I wanted to be forgiving instead of resentful, loving rather than angry, connected and not removed. I wanted to fight my way back to my husband, my family, and myself.

Do not expect immediate results, because this path is a long one. I have purposely made this book easy to carry around and look to whenever you need to be reminded of your strength. I encourage you to highlight passages that resonate with you and use this as a guide. You should make this title as much about your journey as it is about mine.

I was once where you sit right now. I know how it feels

to fester in resentment and hate the person you're lying next to every night. I know what it's like to be disgusted by your husband's touch and not believe you could ever love him again. I thought about running away. I was even attracted to other men simply because I was so starved for connection and intimacy.

This once crossed my mind: "Maybe my husband will hit a tree on his ski trip and pass away. That would make my choice easier." I'm ashamed to say that on one occasion I uttered those words to a friend jokingly. I still find it hard to believe that I was once a person who would think something so horrible. That should tell you more about where I was mentally. I've learned how easily anger transforms people. Festering in that pain for ten years made me a different person. It'd changed me incrementally, over time, so I didn't even realize it was happening. If you are operating from a place of rage and hurt feelings, you are inevitably spreading your agony to others.

It took me a long time to finally feel like I was making progress. Eight months into our relationship rehab, my husband and I were sitting on the couch when I noticed a feeling I didn't recognize. For the first time, I felt content. It was like ten years of resentment had finally been released. Our work was far from done, but it was proof that something new was emerging. I was closer to who I wanted to be, and more removed from the negativity I had reared for so long.

I know you can do this, for no other reason than that you are taking the time to read my story. Don't underestimate the power you have to transform. Think about how many truly happy marriages you see. It seems like the chances of a union working out these days are pretty slim. Many of us throw away anything that breaks because we have never been taught how to fix it. We've never learned how to fix ourselves. Worse, society tells us "we are who we are," so many of us do not even know we *can* change.

My story is not intended to make anybody feel guilty about wanting to leave, or to convince them to stay with someone who isn't right for them. I want to help save your marriage if you know your spouse is a great human being, and if *you know* you would rather rebuild what you have with them than get a divorce. I want to help save your marriage if you recognize that you're in a rut and need a different way of thinking about your marital issues.

Some of you may be so blinded by your inner turmoil that you do not realize you are married to a decent person. Try to put aside your pain for a minute and remember why you fell in love with your husband or wife. If you're still unsure, talk it over with a brutally honest friend or family member. Make sure it's someone you trust, who knows both of you well and will not benefit from your union either way. They may shine some objective light on your situation.

Unless you're married to someone truly toxic and destructive, you can love your spouse again, even if you would rather lie in a bed of fire ants than be with him right now. The only requirement is that you get uncomfortable and explore the choices that have brought you here. You have spent so much time thinking about your spouse's role. It is time that you ask yourself who *you* have been as your marriage deteriorated.

1. MINDSET

People often ask me, "Will my love for my husband ever come back?" Then and there, I know they don't get it. Love isn't "found" like some hidden treasure on a map. Love doesn't return like a beloved pet that got lost when you left the gate open. Love isn't just for the lucky. Love is something you create and cultivate, like a garden. I made a choice to replant myself in different soil and tend to my marriage with respect and commitment.

This story is about the choices my husband and I made that allowed our marriage to break and enabled us to put the pieces back together. It was crucial that we believed we could change, because if we could evolve, then our relationship could, too.

You may expect this book to be a quick fix for your

marital problems. The modern world demands instant gratification. Our culture desperately anesthetizes pain and avoids accountability. Just look at our consumption habits, from food, alcohol, and drugs to materialism. We are a society numbing its pain, thinking we can fill the void with something external. I see it every day in my work. Few are willing to change their lives even if it means better relationships and optimal health. That is an attitude you must discard for this process to work.

We are victims of our genetics, our spouses, our parents, and our circumstances. And if we are casualties instead of active participants, then we do not have to change. We seek to blame, rather than understand, because it enables our behavior. ("It's not my fault. They made me do it! I can't help it.") As a certified health and lifestyle coach, it strikes me how one person can react with rage when offered empowering advice, while someone else with the same prognosis might say, "Please tell me more!"

Some people cringe at the thought of contributing to their own suffering, while others relish the power that understanding gives them. If I play a role in this problem, then I can fix it. If I am a victim, then I am helpless but no change is required. Too many of us would rather throw away our health, and even our relationships, than alter ourselves. There is no easy solution to healing our systems.

Yet when people heal, societies do too. True recovery requires focus and takes time but delivers far better results than any shortcut.

Rescuing a failing relationship begins with understanding how our brains operate when we're in love. Many mistakenly believe that love is the euphoria we feel at the beginning of a relationship when we are invigorated by passion and can't get enough of the other person. That is a stage of love best known for its inebriating chemical reactions, which may explain why we refer to sexual attraction as "chemistry."

When we first fall in love, we are dosed with a biological cocktail of dopamine, norepinephrine (adrenaline), and serotonin designed to drive our focus to one person. This stage can be unstable and highly intoxicating. Not surprising, since those chemicals are also associated with addiction, obsessive compulsive disorder, and (wait for it) temporary insanity!

While at Rutgers University, biological anthropologist Dr. Helen Fisher concluded that there are three stages of love in a relationship. The first is lust, the second is romantic attraction, and the third is attachment. We can all relate to the first two stages. Many believe that those feelings are "true love," I suspect because they are the most pleasurable. However, these stages are not designed for sustainability. Healthy bonds will evolve past these over-stimulating phases.

For the purpose of understanding marriage and long-term relationships, what matters is the final stage that Dr. Fisher calls "attachment." That is when our bodies produce oxytocin, vasopressin, and endorphins. Endorphins are hormones that provide relief from pain and stress. Oxytocin, also known as the "love hormone," plays a role in social bonding, trust, security, sexual reproduction, and childbirth. It will come as no surprise to fellow dog lovers that a 2017 study from Linkoping University in Sweden explains the strong social bond between dogs and humans as being caused by the hormone oxytocin, too.[1]

Research conducted by C. Sue Carter, Ph.D., at Indiana University, found that vasopressin and oxytocin "appear to support autonomic and emotional peak experience such as falling in love, orgasm, and dealing with an initial exposure to a baby."[2] Together, they regulate social, emotional, and adaptive behaviors and create a sense of security and safety. Researchers believe the fluctuating effects of oxytocin and vasopressin explain "why passionate love fades as attachment grows."[3] Combined, these hormones put our bodies into a calmer state.

As you can see, so much of our emotions are regulated by things we can't see, much less control. Before you blindly follow your emotions, you should understand their biological purpose in our brains. Humans operate with three distinct brains. The limbic brain is the chemical and emotional system. The cerebellum is the reptilian mind in the back of our head where habits, passive functions like breathing, and your identity shack up. Then there is the neocortex, which is the big walnut part everyone visualizes when they picture a brain. This outer tissue is the most evolved part of our brain, where intention, decisions, and self-awareness are born. When you lose your shit at your kid's soccer game, or mindlessly eat an entire cake, you are *not* utilizing your Neo C.

Too many of us let our primal brains rule our school. We act on feelings rather than observing from the more evolved part of ourselves. We live without intention or self-awareness. This is the real reason you feel powerless. You are not using the part of your brain with the ability to create a new you. Your life reflects the brain you use most. You will either be reactive, emotional, and fixed in your patterns, or you can be proactive, curious, and focused on growth. You can live impulsively or deliberately. The choice is yours.

I'm asking you to step outside of your compulsions and perceive them as separate from you. Look on them without judgment. Assume the role of a kind, curious, and emotionally neutral best friend.

Equally necessary to this process is understanding love as a verb. When we first fell for someone, we could attribute the fuzzy feelings to chemicals racing through our veins like a drug. Yet we also acted on those feelings. We spent time together, wrote love notes, had sex often, and did things for one another. Our hormones produced thoughts, which led to behaviors that bonded us to another person. If we had kept up with those actions, we would not be where we are today. Once we enter the commitment stage of love, we have to work harder to keep those feelings (and chemicals) going. Admit it, you've gazed into your dog's eyes more than your husband's lately!

You didn't get to this place of resentment overnight, and it will take more than one day to reverse it. Change is disruptive, and something you should learn to embrace. Instead of thinking "I'm uncomfortable and don't like this," think "This is painful, and through this pain I will rise." In order to change, you need to use your rational brain, the neocortex, to outfox the primitive, habit-driven one. Your Neo C. is your ally, your strength, and your higher self. You have it, and it's about flipping time that you used it.

By now, you understand that your mind is where transformation begins. It's the organ that assesses your reality and gets your body to react. Think about your last scary or even sexual dream. There wasn't a physical experience, but your heart beat faster and your body produced all of the same chemicals as if the encounter was real. That is the power of your brain. To it, thought is reality. That's a good thing for our purposes. It means when you alter your beliefs, your emotional responses will follow. And when your feelings shift, your behaviors do, too.

Like learning a new language, this process will be difficult and will require deliberate focus. At first, you will need reminders. You will make mistakes, and you will revert to familiar patterns. You may take two steps forward and one step back. You must embrace the challenge and learn to be conscious of your thoughts in order to change them. Let this book be your guide.

2. IN THE BEGINNING

t was my freshman year at Union College in Schenectady, New York, and I was on campus for preseason soccer a few weeks before the semester started. The place was a ghost town apart from fellow athletes dragging their aching, electrolyte-deficient bodies. I was in the middle of soccer triple sessions and cursing the day I chose the top bunk. Never in my years of competitive sports had I experienced such sore muscles.

My roommate Liz and I were watching television in a common room after soccer practice one day. She was the first to notice the tall football player who quietly sat down behind us, a few couches from the back of the room. I was still glued to the television, oblivious to his presence. All of a sudden, Liz leaned toward my shoulder and slyly but strongly squeezed my biceps.

"Ouch!" I gnarled, not taking my eyes off *Days of Our Lives.*

"You *have* to see the cute guy behind us," she whispered.

Annoyed, but curious to see who could get the jaded Liz so giddy, I slowly turned my head, narrowly avoiding her *don't-be-so-obvious* elbow to the rib cage. I turned around again, slightly disappointed.

"Oh, Liz, he's not *that* cute," I said, more interested in the antics of Bo and Hope.

Not long after, the rest of the student body arrived on campus and Union College was in full swing. Liz soon discovered that Mario was taken, by his first love and high school sweetheart. Far from turning her away, this juicy detail only made him more alluring.

The girlfriend issue did nothing to discourage my pal. From there on out, Liz was Nancy Drew. She found out his name and where he lived on campus—a quad in Fox Hall, the dorm next to ours. She learned he was a freshman football player from Connecticut with three roommates, all from the same state and all hockey players. We were stuck sharing a dorm room, so I endured her new infatuation, though not without my share of eye-rolling.

Mario's dorm room was a frequent stop on our way to late-night fraternity parties, so Liz had plenty of opportunity to pry. Liz used these crowded social events as a way to test her breaking-and-entering skills. She would often pull me into Mario's empty bedroom to snoop while everyone else was in the common room.

What we found earned Mario a fair amount of teasing. Don't worry, if my husband could take it in college, he can take it now. This 18-year-old man had a shrine of his high school girlfriend, complete with teddy bear, heart-shaped sterling silver locket, and multiple-photo picture frame that included a photo of her as a baby. I'd never seen anything like it in any college dorm. I'm pretty sure it's still stored in a box in my attic. It was too endearing to throw away.

Mario proudly displayed this monument of his devotion. While every guy mocked, every girl swooned—including Liz. I was an unwilling accomplice to an illegal search of his desk for one of his girlfriend's letters. I humored Liz's crush, which soon faded. Our group of girls and Mario's gang of guys eventually became one big clan.

Mario and I quickly became close friends. He was funny, kind, honest, and trustworthy. It wasn't long before I allowed him to play matchmaker.

Mario knew one of his roommates was interested in

me and not-so-subtly let me know about it. I still remember us standing together in a group at the ZBT fraternity bar. Mario was bobbing his head to an AC/DC song and kept looking at me while nodding his head toward Dave. His nudging worked. Dave was cute and nice, and we became a serious, though tumultuous, couple on and off for the next three years.

I spent a lot of time with Mario via Dave. They lived in the same quad and whenever Mario's girlfriend visited from Dennison, the four of us would hang out in their suite. I still remember us guarding the bathroom door for each other on the all-male floor.

Freshman year came and went, and so did the high school girlfriend. Mario and Dave rushed the same fraternity but were never roommates again, though we stayed a tight-knit group of friends. I never thought of Mario as anything but a good friend and a pain in the ass. He drove me bonkers with his incessant teasing. He knew exactly how to get under my skin and got punched for it—a lot. Yet he also knew how to make me laugh.

Union College only had about 2,500 students, so there wasn't much opportunity to hide indiscretions. I knew Mario was a good guy because I'd watched him grow up. I saw how he treated girls, how he conducted himself even when alcohol flowed freely at parties, and how he engaged with friend or foe. His behavior was always impeccable. Everyone who knew him respected him. Mario was the kind of guy that any girl in her right mind would want to marry.

In October of our senior year, a few of us were out at an off-campus bar. Mario and I were both single and feeling uninhibited after a couple of beers. Before that, my official status had always been "in a relationship," so Mario and I had never even flirted.

We were standing at the edge of a cluster of our friends, chatting, laughing, and listening to some R.E.M. song streaming from the speakers overhead. Suddenly, the music seemed to fade and we stood alone (or at least it felt that way). He looked at me and said, "I am going to give you the kiss of your life at graduation."

I wasn't sure whether to believe him at first. Ever the ridiculous prankster, Mario jokingly referred to himself as the "kissing bandit" while he was single. He might have said this to any girl standing next to him that night. Yet it felt significant that he mentioned graduation. It meant he still considered me off-limits, given my history with his friend. The beer had created an unusual boldness within me, and I replied, "Why wait?"

He seemed as taken aback as I was by what had escaped from my mouth. Suddenly the music returned full force, and we were once again surrounded by a crowd. It was clear we were both uncomfortable with how intimate the conversation had become. My face warmed, and we nervously backed away, disappearing into the safety of our crowd of friends.

The next day, I was doing my usual run around the campus perimeter when Mario pulled up beside me in his silver GTI. He slowed to a crawl and cranked the passenger side window down while I continued to run. I felt the heat rush to my face and my mouth form a shy smile.

"Cindy!" I scolded myself. "What is happening? This is *Mario*. It's too weird!"

"Do you remember what you said to me last night?" Mario yelled, smirking. This was quintessential Mario—embarrass and tease.

"Of course I remember," I said coyly, while screaming inside. *What is wrong with you? You can't even blame alcohol this time.*

A week later, he walked me home from a fraternity party and really did give me the kiss of my life, all over my apartment, for what seemed like hours. I will spare my kids the details, but it was intense. Let's say we both knew after that night that we could be together for the rest of our lives.

3. WHERE THINGS WENT WRONG

F ast forward to 2012. My husband was at work, and our two boys were at school. I found myself at my kitchen counter alone, typing "how do I stop hating my husband?" into a search bar. I was desperate to release a decade of festering resentment. I was on a fast track to divorce, consumed by a state of suffering I knew was unsustainable. If the internet didn't have answers, at least it might make me feel less alone.

My search came up empty. It would take more than a Google search to solve a decade's worth of marital problems.

Mario and I moved in together right after college and were a good couple through the early stages of our marriage. Moving in wasn't a question of commitment. Both of us were extremely practical about money, so living together just made sense.

We loved our new adult life together. Our first apartment was close to Boston, where we both found jobs shortly after graduation. We adopted a sweet black kitty with yellow eyes that loved to fetch crumpled-up balls of paper. Mario worked from 7 a.m. to 3 p.m. on a construction site, so his day ended earlier than mine. I remember coming home to find him lying on the couch with the cat draped around his neck like a scarf. They were adorable. On weekends, we would go out to dinner, the movies, or to see friends. When the crappy Massachusetts weather permitted, I trained for marathons while Mario played golf on the weekends.

We were engaged in June of 1995 and married a year later. By then, we'd known each other for eight years, dated for five of them, and lived together for four. Within two years, we took the huge step of buying our first home. We loved every charming part of our little white Cape Cod-style house with black shutters. We didn't care that it sat on a major roadway and felt like the inside of a blender every time an 18-wheeler drove through. The busy route out front stood in contrast to the peace we found in the back. There was barely a manmade structure in sight, just a small backyard pond and endless trees that turned gold, orange, and red in the fall. Practical as ever, we planned to have children around age thirty, knowing we would need to save aggressively before we could afford it.

Throughout these changes, life remained new and exciting. We loved our jobs, had great friends, and generally felt fulfilled. Our similar personalities made living together easy. We both liked a clean house, kept our finances organized, and spent responsibly. Neither of us was big on partying, so many nights were spent snuggling our cat and going to bed early—which suited us fine. We liked the same things, lived the same way, and it worked well for a time.

I could trace my unhappiness back to the birth of our second child, Andrew. I quit my job to care for our two children full time. Now the only breadwinner, Mario was working a lot. I had been making good money when we had our first baby, so it was a big adjustment to drop an entire salary while adding another mouth. That wasn't quite the way I saw it, however.

At the time, I was furious that Mario never got up in the middle of the night to change a diaper or rock the babies back to sleep because he had to go to work and I didn't. I was also nursing, so it didn't make sense to him for us both to lose sleep. He went to the gym every morning and came home to a cooked meal every night. I can't count the number of times I stood there watching him eat as I dealt with the babies, feeling ravenous but unable to serve myself until the children were fed. Two kids hardly made a dent in his lifestyle, but they totaled mine.

I was disappointed that he wasn't the doting husband and father I'd imagined he would be, nor was I the joyful, emotionally connected mother and wife I'd envisioned. I missed my work. I missed talking to adults, feeling important, and using my mind to solve problems. We were no longer the fairy tale couple that lived happily ever after. The childrearing stage threw our organized, Type A universe into a whole new reality.

I've always been self-reliant to a fault. I handled problems instead of asking for help and prided myself on being resourceful. While my independence made me productive in a career, it turned out to be my greatest weakness in marriage and motherhood.

After my kids were born, my life revolved around laundry, diapers, groceries, cleaning the house, and keeping the kids alive. I was juggling every soccer ball, baseball, and hockey puck all at once. It wasn't about enjoying time with my children or getting on the floor to play. It was always about the next chore. I look back now and cringe at the time I lost because I couldn't be present.

I rarely asked my husband for help, and why would I?

He had eyes. He made it clear that his hands were full at work and he didn't have the bandwidth for anything else. As usual, I refused to be a burden. In reality, I didn't know how to ask for assistance. I was convinced needing support was a sign of weakness. This self-awareness was non-existent back then, however. The realizations came much, much later, and I am still learning to listen to them.

My marriage took a turn for the worse in May 2004. This was when my resentment went from a hot simmer to boiling over. Many of us live in a kind of limbo, repeating our daily patterns until something causes us to snap. This can be a good change or a bad one. In the following moment, I made a pain-filled choice.

My one-year-old had a severe stomach bug and hadn't been able to keep food down for three days. My three-year-old had had the same issue a day before, and the night before that, I was praying to the porcelain god myself.

It was 5 a.m. I was exhausted from puking my brains out, but all I could think about was my starving baby. Desperation outweighed pride, and for the first time, I asked my husband to stay home to help me get Andrew to eat. I told him that if Andrew couldn't keep his breakfast down, we'd have to take him to the emergency room. My husband looked me dead in the eyes and said, "I have to go to spin class." He felt "fat" after a week in Florida eating and drinking crap with his golf buddies.

"The gym is ten minutes away," he assured me, grabbing his car keys. "So I'm close if there's an issue."

I said nothing, slipping into silence as I always did to avoid confrontation. He didn't want me to need him, so I didn't want to need him either. This attitude alone is a marriage killer. In that moment, I decided that I would never ask anything from my husband again. In making that decision, I shut down any way for Mario to redeem himself. No matter what he did or how he changed after that point, it didn't matter. I'd shut the door on our relationship.

After my husband left for the gym, Andrew ate like it was his first meal after a long hibernation, only to erupt in a volcano of applesauce and oatmeal. Fear gripped my heart as his body spewed its only source of nourishment for days.

I scooped the boys up in their matching green-and-navy Hanna Andersson pajamas and drove to a nearby hospital. A mess in sweatpants and Coke-bottle glasses, I watched anxiously as Andrew bypassed everyone in the ER and was instantly hooked up to an IV. The nurse quietly took me aside and cautiously put her hand on my shoulder.

"Are you alone, dear?" she whispered.

With angry tears, I replied, "My husband had to go to a *fucking* spin class."

That May morning, my one-year-old son was admitted to the hospital for three days and I emotionally vacated my marriage for the next ten years. That day also marked my newfound love and appreciation of the F-word.

Years later, after we'd moved from Boston to Texas, my husband resurfaced as the wonderful man I had married and apologized for being so selfish. He admitted he got caught up in himself and did not know how to meet everyone's needs. Mario tried his hardest to bring me back to him, but neither of us realized how far gone I really was.

I'd spent years building those walls, and I wasn't ready to take them down. My armor had allowed me to mask the problems instead of dealing with them. It'd also made me immune to his remorse. In my mind, it was his fault I couldn't trust him with my heart. He deserved my indifference. I didn't want to forgive my husband. I didn't want to love him again. Back then I would have said "I can't" love him again. The truth was I wouldn't.

This is a choice too many people make. We are reluctant to forgive, though we want to be exonerated for our own mistakes. Humans can be so insufferably righteous. We play this black-and-white virtue game and expect others to be perfect when we aren't ourselves. We lose our ability to empathize and feel disconnected because people let us down. Yet we only poison ourselves. My anger festered for so long that it became part of me. Encased in my armor, my personality became even more rigid and uptight.

Through it all, I remained a dutiful wife and mother even as I seethed inside. Pain cannot survive inside of you for long. Eventually it transforms into something else. I desperately dug a hole for my suffering, hoping to bury it. There was just one problem. You cannot isolate the bad from the good. When you close yourself off to painful emotions, you block out the pleasant ones too, leaving yourself numb and indifferent.

I learned the hard way that the opposite of love is not hate, but indifference. For years I was shut down, void of any feelings toward my husband. This would lead me to a vulnerable and dangerous place. Festering resentment creates a darkness within us. Left unchecked, it will lead us farther from our best self. More than once, I found myself in situations that set off all the warning signs in my head. Flirting is easy and feels really *good* when you are desperate for the connection you have deliberately severed from your spouse. I look back now and shudder to think of what I could have lost forever if I had gone farther.

Nothing changed until we moved to Texas and my kids

started school full time. That's when I decided to pursue a nutrition and health coaching certification. I soon realized food and health was less about calories, fat, protein, and carbs than how we are living as a society. My eyes opened to a whole new way of understanding. I saw a population that was stressed, anxious, and running on autopilot. A culture that throws away the broken instead of trying to fix it.

Like many people, I thought I was incredibly insightful because I could explain *why* I acted the way I did. Yet I often used defeatist language:

"I've always been this way."

"This is just who I am."

"People don't change."

"My parents or upbringing made me like this."

Do any of those sound familiar? These explanations gave me permission to stay the same. There are many ways people avoid facing the truth. Some, like me, will deny we can change. Others may prefer to put on a façade of a perfect life. Yet whether we pretend to understand our issues or stick our heads in the sand, the result is the same. There can be no evolution.

Through my health rewiring, I recognized the pervasive victim mentality that America had adopted. Like many people, I blamed anything and everything outside of myself. I told myself I was no fun as a mother and wife because my husband was not there for me when I needed him most.

For years, I believed my husband made me this way. I was the one who tried to do everything right. Who has time to be fun when there's so much to do and nobody to help me?

We use stories to justify our own undesirable behavior, which contributes to the epidemic of emotionally stunted adults. We are miserable because we don't want to adjust. We'd rather deflect blame than get uncomfortable. We like our stories and we're sticking with them!

With my marriage, I was so focused on my own suffering that I could not appreciate everything I had. I couldn't see the good I was pushing away, nor the bad I was drawing into my life. I only felt justified in my anger. Meanwhile, I believed I was a good wife and mother for attending to my duties despite my unhappiness.

No one ever told me that gratitude and happiness were the most important qualities to cultivate as a human being. As a society, we put much less value on joy than we do on productivity or even the appearance of it. We acquire every milestone the world tells us will make us happy, then we wonder what went wrong when happiness isn't suddenly delivered.

How did it feel the last time someone held a mirror up to your actions or gave you constructive criticism? Many people find comfort in ignorance and disquiet in truth. Some become angry with anyone who dares to hold them accountable. Yet freedom and creativity cannot exist without the ability to fail and redirect.

> *"The trouble with most of us is that we would rather be ruined by praise than saved by criticism."*
>
> – Norman Vincent Peale

Many of us run from our own liberation because it requires taking responsibility. It puts us in a position where we must face our mistakes. Most of us would rather focus on the culpability of others. We see ourselves as the good guys in every situation, no matter what role we played. We will do terrifying feats of mental gymnastics to justify our own missteps, and yet grant no such vindication to others. We tell ourselves that we have *reason* to behave badly and therefore aren't really bad. Then we feel affronted when others slip up, as if they have no excuse.

We create our own suffering with the meaning we apply to our circumstances. When we experience negative emotions for long periods, we become self-absorbed. *This happened to me, and this is what it means about me. That person did this to me, and this is what it means about me.* This mentality is egotistical at best and, at worst, borderline narcissistic. I want to make this as clear as Saran Wrap. Nothing your husband, mother, relative, or friend did is about you. *It is always about them.*

We all have challenges. The problem arises when we create a negative internal dialogue about those difficulties and choose to wallow in our own misfortune. We can carry hardships on our backs and let them define us, or we can let them go so we can grow. Adversity can weigh us down, or it can be a building block.

The victim mentality is all about ego and protection of the self. If nothing is ever our fault, we never have to do anything different. This idea leaves us both inculpable and impotent. Many of us take on this role because we don't believe we can transform. It also protects us from the discomfort of our evolution.

Through my study of food and health, I transformed the way I ate and lived. The research I did took me down a road less traveled. It taught me to challenge conventional ideas, especially the ones that seem to work for no one. This reformed way of thinking granted me a new lens through which to observe my ten years of marital suffering. The power to change my physical health came from questioning everything I knew about well-being. Now I had to alter how I thought about my marriage.

Einstein once said, "We cannot solve our problems with the same thinking we used when we created them." You cannot solve your marital hitches with the same mindset that led to them. That is why you are here. To challenge the thoughts, beliefs, and stories that got you to this point. My hope is that by the end of this book, you will make the choice to toss out the destructive thoughts instead of your marriage.

When my marriage reached rock bottom, I chose to learn instead of leave. I picked curiosity and communication over my old apathetic ways. I interrogated everything I believed about myself, Mario, and our union to see if I could come up with a more empowering narrative in which I played an active role. Taking responsibility gave me power. How did I do it?

First, I asked how the hell I got to this point. I took inventory of any destructive beliefs that led to damaging choices and behaviors. I acknowledged that my personality and emotions had led me to what was a point of no return for most marriages.

Through this journey, I stopped thinking about how my husband hurt me and questioned how much I'd wrong-ly assumed. How often had I jumped to conclusions without giving him the benefit of the doubt? How many times had I chosen to focus on the bad rather than the good? How ungrateful was I when I clearly had so much to be thankful for?

I *chose* to make motherhood and marriage about chores instead of joy. In doing that, I allowed damaging thoughts and emotions to impact my emotional health for nearly a decade.

When you take responsibility for your life, you're able to respond to it. When you blame outside forces for your problems, there is no way to counter, nor can there be emotional or spiritual evolution. Your growth has stopped, which is why you feel stuck. That horrible stagnant feeling is your call to arms. It is not a curse, but an opportunity to transform.

When I realized that my marriage was teetering, I had to make a choice. Luckily, I had the awareness and strength at that point to make the right decision for myself, which was (and often is!) the hard one.

As a coach, I can tell you that the majority of people will do anything but fix themselves. Questioning your own behaviors and challenging your identity is the highest form of human intelligence. It comes from a willingness to face your shortcomings and admit your mistakes. It will always be the most challenging place to travel, and many would rather live a life of despair than go there.

To save my marriage, I had to dive in, feet first and unarmed. I had to start living honestly and intentionally. This would give me the courage to climb the mountains I needed to conquer within myself.

Throughout this process, you need to remember that love is selfless. You have to be willing to look in the mirror day after day and ask yourself how *you* can be a better person and a better spouse. When you are willing to cry, kick, scream, and fight your way back to someone, that is a sign of true love.

Many people are confused about love. It isn't the wild elation you feel when you first fall for someone. The beginning is the easy part. Love is what you do when everything sucks, you are miserable, and the shit has hit the Big Ass Fan. I am proud to say that my husband and I are capable of that type of love.

I chuckle now when after a full day's work, my husband tells me to sit down while he does the dishes, and I'll say, "No, honey, you've been so stressed. You go sit down." Now we fight to help each other. Boy, how times have changed!

"How do I stop hating my husband?" is the wrong question. You can love your husband or you can hate him, but you cannot "stop hating" him.

To move away from hate, we have to engage in love. To engage means to attract. You can engage in love. You can engage in gratitude. You can engage in joy. They all come from your most exposed, authentic and vulnerable self.

What you engage in and focus on will grow. When I stopped concentrating on why I hated my husband and started remembering why I fell in love with him, our feelings and marriage started to bloom again.

Love is a choice. Every thought in your head, every emotion in your body, every behavior you exhibit is a choice. Apathy is also a choice. Hate is a choice. Shifting blame is a choice. Taking responsibility for your life is your choice.

In the following chapters, I will explain the exact steps that I took to transform myself and my marriage, while changing every aspect of my life in the process.

10 STEPS TO TRANSFORMATION

"Transformation is a journey of discovery."

– Rick Warren

1. *Define your values* - What are your values? Be specific. What character traits do you desire in a spouse? Does your spouse demonstrate those characteristics?

2. *Decide* - The first step to loving your spouse and saving your marriage is deciding to love your spouse and save your marriage.

3. *Change your story* – Rewrite the story of your relationship so that you may have a different ending.

4. *Be present* - You must be present to be aware and appreciative.

5. *Be grateful* - Cultivate an attitude of gratitude to improve your life.

6. *Love yourself* - Believe in your ability to transform and step into new possibilities.

7. *Manifest what you want* - Act on your hopes instead of your fears.

8. *Think about your thinking* - Understand how your mind works so you can think and act with purpose.

9. *Engage* - Adjust the way you act, and your feelings will follow.

10. *Reset your mindset* - Get curious about the beliefs that are limiting you.

4. DEFINE YOUR VALUES

"Keep your thoughts positive because your thoughts become your words. Keep your words positive because your words become your behavior. Keep your behavior positive because your behavior becomes your habits. Keep your habits positive because your habits become your values. Keep your values positive because your values become your destiny."

– Mahatma Gandhi

Having strong values shows the standards that you demand of yourself and enforces accountability. Values are a person's principles, their judgment of what is important in life. They form the basis of our character. It's easier to make decisions when you know what is important.

As I contemplated divorce, the two ideals that harassed me the most were commitment and health. I remembered when Mario and I put all of our money together and bought our first little home in Wayland, Massachusetts. The living room had a beautiful fireplace and there was dark wood everywhere that we couldn't wait to paint white. It was a huge job that required sanding and many annoying coats of Kilz before painting could even start.

When Mario went to Peru for a week to visit his parents, I nearly sanded my fingerprints off getting the job done to surprise him when he got back. Every day, I took the train into Boston for work, then came home and painted past midnight. I would've stayed up all night if it was necessary. That's how determined I was to make that room white like we'd imagined together.

Commitment, or never quitting, was one of my core values. My marriage was arguably the most important commitment I'd ever made. Yet I was actually considering giving it up. I thought about all of the goals I'd set for myself and stuck with until the end. I'd figured out how to get over every hurdle in my path.

"This is your ultimate test, your biggest obstacle yet,"

Commitment told me. "This is where you prove what you are made of."

Commitment had been my friend for a long, long time, and she was not going to let me let her go without a fight. That's the beauty of having clear values. They hold you accountable when you start to waver.

Then there was my core value of good health. Health, to me, is not just about eating vegetables and working out, it's about learning and personal growth. Physical health had always been invaluable, but I'd come to learn more about its more complicated emotional side. I realized that no external version of health mattered if my insides were riddled with unwanted emotions.

I ate well, exercised, and was physically healthy, but a negative mindset had hijacked my inner life. Health held up a mirror between Mario and me as if to say, "He is not your problem, *you* are."

Having strong values often means swallowing some brutal honesty, no ego or hypocrisy allowed. I realized that the more I made decisions based on unhappy beliefs, the more negativity I got back. It was clear that I couldn't rely on my emotions to guide me. It was destroying my family and had changed me in ways that did not align with who I wanted to be.

Everything I believed and felt about Mario was

wrapped up in things about me that I did not like. The bad parts of my marriage consumed me. The worst of me and the ugliest parts of our union were a package deal. Many people find themselves here and think the only way to unload their misery is to ditch their spouse. I had a different notion. The marriage sparked my suffering. The anguish, in turn, devoured my marriage like a cancer. I wanted to see if I could target and heal the suffering itself.

When my marriage was on the chopping block, one of the smartest things I did was think about my core values. Commitment reminded me that I was not a quitter. Health urged me to separate from the drama and toxicity that had brought me to this place. My values urged me to seek a different way out. For the first time, I was able to disconnect from the unruly thoughts that had consumed me for years, leading me down this unwanted path.

Many of us let emotions act on our behalf, not realizing feelings are not always intelligent or even sane. I recognized that I wasn't in the right frame of mind to make monumental choices for myself and my family. A resolution like divorce can have far-reaching implications for everyone involved, from children to in-laws to family friends. When the stakes are that high, you don't want to react emotionally. Decisions, especially the important ones, should be tethered to our values and not our feelings in the moment.

There are people who should leave their spouse but don't, and there are people who belong with their partner and quit anyway. I have seen both, and I need to reiterate that this book is only *my* story. I want to share how I came back to my marriage in order to give hope to those who need it. I am not encouraging you to stay in a situation that is bad for you. I certainly don't mean to shame anybody for choosing differently than I did.

Just take a moment to self-reflect before making any major life choices. That's all I'm saying. When I dug deep inside, I was haunted by that memory of my husband and our first home. I have no idea why that instance of commitment came into my head, but it worked. My values gave me the clarity of thought that my emotions had obscured.

Mario and I shared a long history. We had a beautiful family, mutual friends we loved, and the same values. We shared an adoration for food and dogs. Though I did not feel strong love toward Mario at that time, I also realized he was still the man I wanted to marry. Despite his mistakes, he was a decent human being who was open to growth and, therefore, capable of change. He had already demonstrated that to me.

These positive thoughts were a shift for me. They only

became available because I separated from the emotional turmoil smothering me like hot fudge on vanilla ice cream. Your thinking will change once you separate from your emotional baggage. Start to recognize that your emotional baggage is not part of you. It's just an unnecessary carry-on.

I strongly advise thinking about your spouse's character before you rush a decision you can't take back. There must be a reason you once loved him. If he is a good person who shares similar values, you can save this, *if* you want to.

What about infidelity? I get questions about this all the time on my blog, usually from women involved in an emotional or physical affair. I've also gotten messages from men whose wives have strayed, many who are desperate to win her back despite the cheating.

My answer is the same whether you or your spouse is guilty. I know both good people and awful people who have made mistakes and crossed these lines. I realize saying this can set people off like Fourth of July fireworks. You may be thinking there is no such thing as a "good person that cheats," and you are correct. No one is being a good person when they cheat.

In my fifty years of life, I have come to understand that people are not simply good or bad. Our character is not etched in stone. With any mistake, we have control over our response to it. All of us can change, for better or for worse. Life is a slippery slope. There are many rabbit holes to fall down, especially when we (often unknowingly) act from a negative emotional state. We are all one choice away from changing the trajectory of our lives. Choice is truly that simple, and that powerful.

Human beings are meant to learn, grow, and evolve. We fuck up, sometimes royally. This is usually the result of past damage and is often exacerbated by a self-destructive internal monologue. I say it all the time: Hurt people hurt people. I try to focus on the behavior and not the person. When behavior is bad, it can be corrected. We may be defined by our choices, but we can make different ones.

When a human being is labeled as bad, it's implied that they can never change. Society tends to shame people for their mistakes instead of helping them improve. That's because it's easier to judge than to self-correct. Why do we tend to believe someone is a bad person instead of believing that they made a bad choice?

I've often wondered if these beliefs also perpetuate bad behavior. People who are shamed into thinking they are inherently bad cannot separate from their past behavior. Instead of moving on from their mistakes, they fall deeper, becoming even more damaged and destructive. Shaming is an invitation to misery and paralysis. Distinguishing bad behavior from bad people is critical.

Our character is malleable, which means we must aspire to uphold it every single day. You could go from being a liar to being an honest person in one day, simply by choosing to start telling the truth. You can go from honest to deceitful, or resentful to forgiving, with just one choice. Every day our character is challenged, and our decisions determine who we become.

A lifetime of exploration into human behavior has shown me there is a fine line between good and bad people. I believe in innate goodness, mine and others', as well as our ability to change. Understanding the difference between "behavior" and "being" directly affects our capacity to forgive others and transform ourselves.

I have given you a lot to think about in this first step. Take some time to dissect your thoughts. I am not telling you to stay with someone who has betrayed you, nor are cheaters automatically unworthy. We must always hold ourselves and other people accountable for behavior. It can be helpful to explore the person's choices and life. For example, was the betrayal part of a larger, recurring pattern? Many serial cheaters do not just cheat on their spouse. Their dishonesty may appear in other parts of their life. That's because recurrent cheating creates a web of lies and involves near constant deceit. You might notice it in their business practices or with their friends. Infidelity is clearly a very sensitive topic, and there is no absolute way of knowing who is worthy of forgiveness and who is not. That is a personal choice.

"Define your values" also means you need to determine what is most important to you. Reflect on the character traits you wish to embody and those you want in a partner. When I took a step back and identified my values, I knew that my husband was still very much the man I wanted. I also recognized a need to cultivate change within myself to be the person I wanted to be.

5. DECIDE

"Love is a decision, it is a judgment, it is a promise. If love were only a feeling, there would be no basis for the promise to love each other forever. A feeling comes and it may go. How can I judge that it will stay forever, when my act does not involve judgment and decision?"

– Erich Fromm

I watched my husband pace back and forth from my perch on our living room couch. The complete and total destruction of our marriage lay between us, and we had to decide our next steps. Would we divorce? Separate for a while?

I was petrified, knowing that apathy was no longer an option. We could no longer tread water in the ocean of denial. We were drowning in every bad decision we had made in our relationship. My heart was beating outside my chest. I feared what would come next. I could feel my body surge with adrenaline and cortisol. I had managed to avoid this decision for years. Divorce was never the plan, but neither was a loveless marriage.

Now we stood at a crossroads. Were we the type to work through the pain or run away? Could we forgive without residual blame? Can emotional health be restored to an unhealthy union? Can two people really fall back in love?

In that moment, I didn't know what I wanted. I did know what I *didn't* want, so I started there. I knew I did not want to be divorced. I did not want my children to shuttle back and forth between two houses every week-end, birthday, and holiday. I also knew that invisible link to my husband would never end even after the kids grew up. There would be graduations, weddings, and grandchildren, then the holidays and birthday cycle for the little ones all over again.

My own parents got divorced after thirty-seven of years of marriage, so I knew how it could impact even adult children. I know that dull haze it casts over family reunions. I know the heartache that children feel when the foundation of their life is pulled out from under them. I was already a wife and mother when my parents split, and it still shattered me. I also witnessed friends' divorces and knew it was an unending hell for all involved. If I was going to get divorced, I had to make absolutely sure it was the only way.

I knew my husband was a decent man. I knew we were once very much in love. I knew we had a great life that I'd allowed to be soiled by resentment and pain. I knew that I had made a commitment to this man and to my family, and I had never backed out on a commitment—ever. Was I going to give up on the most important commitment I'd ever made?

Then I thought, "If I cannot make it with this man, with everything we have together, what makes me think I can make it with anyone else?" We had everything we could ask for in a relationship and we still managed to mess it up.

I knew the baggage that brought me here would follow me everywhere if it wasn't unpacked. We all know folks who carry their baggage from one relationship to the next. They keep repeating their mistakes until they finally discover what they are supposed to learn. I understood that I had to unload that weight. I also knew that this man, this marriage, this home, and this family was the safest space for me to do it.

I also knew, no matter what road I chose, it would be the most agonizing and grueling experience of my life. It did not make sense to go through this hardship only to end up losing my family. Surely, I still had a lot to fight for.

So, I knew I did not want divorce, but separation seemed like a possibility. It would give us time to think and clear out any negative emotions.

I flirted with the idea, but Mario felt differently. He thought separation would bring us farther apart and not closer together. Instead, he proposed a couple of conditions for fixing our marriage that seemed selfish to me at the time. He insisted on spending time together, communicating more, holding hands, hugging, and having sex. The fact that we needed "rules" telling us to do these things might give you an idea of where my feelings were.

When your emotional state is at its lowest point, it's a good idea to let someone more stable make decisions. I had enough awareness to realize that I was not in the best mindset. I hated to admit it, but I had to be saved from myself. My husband was in a better condition to respond to our needs. He also knew what he wanted more than I did.

He told me that separation was not an option. We would stay and work at it under these rules, or we would divorce. He also wouldn't wait around for me to think about it. I had to decide immediately. He wouldn't allow us to take time apart. His theory was simple. Distance would create distance, not closeness.

I could not argue with his logic. We could not fix our relationship by walking away from each other. We could not face our problems by avoiding them. We could not put us back together if we chose to break apart. And Lord knows we couldn't just try. We had to decide. This is how I learned the secret to a happy marriage. It is remarkably, unbelievably, and frustratingly simple.

The most important step to loving my husband and saving my marriage was *deciding* to love my husband and save my marriage.

Everything in life comes down to our choices. "Trying" to fix your marriage is not a choice. Trying is a way out. It's an excuse in case you change your mind. We try on clothes to see if they fit. We try new foods to see if we like them. Trying is a great thing under certain circumstances, but it is not good enough for the most important decisions in our lives.

Imagine someone saying "I'm going to try that new diet," instead of "I'm changing my eating habits and life-style." Or "I'm trying to write a book," versus "I am writing a book." It's the difference between "We are trying to fix our marriage" and "We are fixing our marriage." Trying is just another form of indecision. It sets the groundwork for failure, because we aren't committed to the outcome.

To fix your marriage, you and your spouse must decide to fix your marriage. And when you will not accept any other outcome, I promise you will get the marriage that you want.

"Do, or do not. There is no try."

– Yoda

6. CHANGE YOUR STORY

"Is your life story the truth? Yes, the chronological events are true. Is it the whole truth? No, you see and judge it through your conditioned eyes and mind—not of all involved—nor do you see the entire overview. Is it nothing but the truth? No, you select, share, delete, distort, subtract, assume and add what you want, need and choose to."

— Rasheed Ogunlaru

Our heads are filled with stories we tell ourselves about life, our relationships, and the world. These tales are manufactured unconsciously and yet they dictate our actions. Our worst stories are born out of pain and fear, and often they aren't even true.

Narratives help us understand the world, but sometimes they can misconstrue reality. The key to changing the sagas we tell ourselves is to become curious about them. Dissect them like the frog in your eighth-grade biology class. Ask yourself what is factual and what is based on opinion. If you cannot tell the difference between a fact and a belief, you will never know truth.

The only fact in my story was that my husband did not help me when my kids were babies, and this hurt me. I *believed* that he didn't help because he did not love us, or he did not care when he saw me struggling. I never gave him the opportunity to tell me what his actions really meant. I just assumed I knew.

I never considered, for example, that his way of showing love was working hard to provide for us. It didn't occur to me that he might see me as a supermom who'd never needed help before. After all, I'd never asked for it. I'd literally made Wonder Woman my avatar. I was proud of my self-reliance and often referred to myself as the "most productive mom in the world." I can see how that would deter my husband from encroaching on my turf.

Now, I am not saying it was all in my head and my husband was a saint. I am saying that marriage and raising kids are hard, and both parties will screw up. I had to recognize there were times I may have misinterpreted what was going on. Every wrong assumption I made in our marriage rode in on the back of those initial misunderstandings. There were many little stories of being let down by my husband that snowballed into the chronicle of our marriage. All of it could be whittled down to blame, victimhood, and misshapen beliefs.

Stories allow us to avoid admitting that we need to do better. We have excuses for why our marriage sucks, why we are unhealthy, or why we are unhappy. We have justifications for why we don't do what we should, or why we do the things we know we shouldn't.

For years, I told myself that my husband was the jerk in our duo. "He wasn't there for me when I needed him. I tried hard to be the best mother and wife that I could, and he did not put in the same effort. I put up with it for longer than should be expected of me."

This myth gave me permission to be bitter, which manifested in our daily life as passive aggressive commentary. It also allowed me to act even more uptight and rigid. In my mind, the children's well-being was on my shoulders alone. I was a martyr fulfilling the duties of mother and wife without complaint. I stopped thinking about myself or what I wanted, focusing instead on what I accomplished and how it looked to the outside.

I thought it was important to have dinner on the table every night. I didn't think my children needed to see me laugh or have fun. It was easy to just check things off my list and value accomplishments I could clearly see and tally. I didn't realize that my emotional state spoke louder than any color-coded spreadsheet.

How you feel is your quality of life. The silly chores did not make me a better mom, wife, or person. They just allowed me to delude myself while I sank deeper into self-inflicted misery. To wrestle with love, pain, vulnerability, anger, guilt, joy, or gratitude is to be alive. I was completely numb. I chose to not deal with or feel any of it. When I finally faced what I'd become, I asked, "Cindy, is this really who you want to be?"

I wanted to be the mom who danced liked a fool at parties and could laugh exuberantly with her kids. I wanted to be a mom who stomped in muddy puddles and sang in the rain. I wanted to be a flirty and fun-loving wife.

To be honest, those traits were out of character for me. They didn't represent who I was, only who I wanted to be. I admired other moms for their creativity and playfulness. Yet I believed that spontaneity was not in my DNA. I was "too type A." I was convinced that my personality was pre-determined and set in stone.

That belief was absolutely and categorically wrong. Nothing about our personality is permanent unless we decide to make it so. Even then, we're only fooling ourselves. It is much easier to say "This is just the way I am" or "I have always been this way." Those are justifications for choosing to *be* instead of choosing to *become*. (We will explore this "fixed mindset" much more later in the book.)

The emotionally stunted Cindy did not choose to fix my marriage. She chose apathy every single day for ten years. The second I chose otherwise, I became a different person, which invited new possibilities into my life. We do not need to cling to the "fixed" story we have about who we are. I'd spent a lifetime looking for proof to support my limiting beliefs and rejecting anything that challenged these ideals. You can bet your bottom dollar that if we do this with our own worthiness, we have likely distorted stories about other people too. We have not yet learned the difference between belief and fact.

I recognized that it was my conditioning, my focus, and my judgments that got me to this point in my marriage. The how and why only affirmed the person I did not want to be and the life I no longer wanted. The distorted tales I wrote destroyed me and my marriage. Yet it also meant that different stories could create a different ending.

I did not have love because I chose hate.

I did not have forgiveness because I chose resentment.

I did not have passion because I chose apathy.

I *chose* perfection over creativity. I *chose* to be angry instead of sexy. I know it seems simplistic, because it is. We get what we choose. You may agree with what I'm telling you but feel tempted to include some caveat for your situation.

"Yes, I did this or that, but only because ..."

As long as you continue to justify your behavior, the door is closed to transforming your situation. As long as you continue with the mindset that got you here, you will keep getting the same circumstances. Let go of ideas that don't serve you, because they are holding you back.

I'm not saying you should assume total responsibility for the downfall of your marriage. The idea is not to blame yourself and redeem your spouse. You are, however, part of the problem and therefore part of the solution. My husband made many mistakes, and so did I. Both of us had to change, but the only story I could rewrite was my own.

I had to accept that my assumptions weren't facts, and they had yielded ten years of the same woeful tale. I never considered that my own conditioning was to blame. I was looking for the bad and deleting the good, shaping my story to leave me vindicated and my husband the villain. Blame robs our power to effect change. My mind was made up about my situation, so everything that happened was viewed through that lens.

When you take responsibility for your story, you can respond to it. This may be difficult for some of us to accept, but it is the only way to evolve. We are responsible for what we believe, which is the precursor to behavior. Our minds frame our reality, dictating what we look for and therefore what we see. Many of us cannot conceptualize this because our minds are closed.

I had to be willing to change my mind. My stories did not bring out the best in me. Yet I gave them the power to affect my relationship. I had to halt the habitual responses and reframe my marriage. I realized I wanted no part of my old belief system, which represented a passive and irresponsible way of existing. So I came up with a new story.

"The moment you accept responsibility
for everything in your life
is the moment you gain the power
to change anything in your life."

– Hal Elrod

7. BE PRESENT

"All negativity is caused by an accumulation of psychological time and denial of the present. Unease, anxiety, tension, stress, worry—all forms of fear—are caused by too much future, and not enough presence. Guilt, regret, resentment, grievances, sadness, bitterness, and all forms of non-forgiveness are caused by too much past, and not enough presence."

– Eckhart Tolle

Conscious choices can only be made in the present. If you live only in the past or the future, you are powerless in the here and now.

Nothing about becoming a parent was what I anticipated. Neither my husband nor I lived up to the expectations I had set in my mind. I was one of those mothers who stressed over every detail. I lived for when my kids would go to sleep so I could put things back in order.

Meanwhile, I had a friend who converted a whole section of her house to an arts and crafts room. Another friend, who didn't have cable television, opted instead to read twenty books to her kids every night. I envied how fun and easygoing they seemed. I longed for their patience and creativity.

It is difficult to be present (or pleasant) when you are always focused on the next chore. I tolerated the finger painting, Play-Doh, and puzzles my children needed for their development, while itching so badly to clean it all up. I couldn't be present because I was too busy being productive. I was still in the mindset of career woman, putting a greater value on productivity than fun. I wasn't the crafty parent, I was the responsible, get-shit-done mom. I had the laundry folded *and* put away. I never took a nap or skipped a workout, and I still had dinner on the table by 7 p.m.

From my pedestal of efficiency, I looked down on friends who spent precious time each night cozily sharing numerous books with their children. I was one book and done, on to the next thing! I imagined that their homes were a sty and their laundry baskets damp and musty. You would never find a pile of smelly clothes in *my* house. I never relaxed or stopped thinking about what I had to do next.

Yet you want to know the truth? I secretly wanted to be those other moms. I focused on areas where I excelled in order to not feel insecure about the parts where I fell dreadfully short.

We are often most judgmental about the things we need to correct in ourselves. Think about what you criticize most harshly in others. That may give you some insight into what you might need to fix within yourself.

I wasn't a neglectful mom, but I wasn't a joyful one either. I lacked balance. I was a career woman before I was a mother, so I applied the only model I knew. As a mother, I was rigid and focused. I had trouble transitioning into my new, softer role as a caretaker of messy, unruly, and unpredictable children. By the time I realized this, the finger-painting days were over.

I didn't learn about mindfulness until I began my journey to better health. When I did, I realized I hated living in the future and being stressed all the time. Even in my own middle school days, I never had fun until my work was done—as if the work was ever truly done. I insisted my friends and I all do our homework before we could watch

Santa Barbara. (Their moms really loved me for that.) Even now, being still is the most arduous exercise for me.

Despite my inexperience, I learned to meditate (though not well). I practiced bringing my awareness to the now and ridding myself of unwanted emotions. Whenever I felt overwhelmed or frustrated, I stopped and named those feelings. I asked what thoughts created those emotions, and whether they served me. I engaged in deep breathing to bring myself back to awareness.

Once I started spending more time in the present, I was able to act more consciously. I realized my incessant focus on the future was overwhelming me. In order to overcome this pattern, I had to remove myself from my emotions so I could reflect on them.

Making Play-Doh with my kids, I was already thinking about the cleanup. I wasn't enjoying my children's creativity. I can't even remember if they made shapes, or turtles, or snakes, because I wasn't present enough to notice. This is how I rolled most of the time, and it took me a long time to realize I could be different.

Presence isn't just noticing our emotions so that we can make deliberate choices. It is about noticing *everything*. This was a welcome side effect that I did not expect. Being more mindful allowed me catch things I never noticed before. The most productive people are usually the last to stop and smell the peonies. We don't have time for it, nor do we think it is worthy of attention.

The stillness is where wonder, awe, and appreciation recreate. I developed this intimate connection with nature I never had before, which has touched my soul in ways that have fundamentally changed me. To see beautiful things that have always been here, just short of my attention, is to move my awareness into a divine realm. This domain is where our greatest selves flourish.

My newfound mindfulness practice made me much more reverent of life itself and naturally led to the next piece of the puzzle. Do you want to know the antidote to all suffering? Turn the page.

8. BE GRATEFUL

"Gratitude, like faith, is a muscle. The more you use it, the stronger it grows, and the more power you have to use it on your behalf. If you do not practice gratefulness, its benefaction will go unnoticed, and your capacity to draw on its gifts will be diminished. To be grateful is to find blessings in everything. This is the most powerful attitude to adopt, for there are blessings in everything."

– Alan Cohen

You don't need a science experiment to prove that you cannot be miserable and grateful at the same time. Many of us have felt the incompatibility.

Gratitude makes people happier, more resilient, more relaxed, and it improves well-being. It increases self-esteem, optimism, health, longevity, productivity, creativeness, and self-awareness.

Yet being grateful often goes against our instincts. Most people would rather complain about what bothers them than expound on an equally small thing that brought them joy. One insult will often stick in our minds longer than five compliments. I had many things to be grateful for, but I lacked practice in appreciating them.

Our minds are the original supercomputer. Every time we add something new, like presence and gratitude, we are upgrading the operating system. I had to supplant my current thinking with new, healthier ways of using the hardware in my head.

What begins as a concerted effort to cultivate gratitude will quickly turn into habit. I appreciate more now without even trying. This goes hand in hand with being more present. You cannot appreciate what you don't notice. That doesn't mean I never get busy or complain, but I try to redirect when I do. Here are a few ideas for incorporating more gratitude into your life right now:

- Journal for five minutes daily, even if it's just jotting down three things you are grateful for.
- Keep a "gratitude jar," and make it a daily prac-

tice for your family. Each morning, have everyone write down one thing they are grateful for and add it to their jar.

- Every time you feel an unhealthy emotion, ask yourself what you can do to cultivate a more positive response right now.

- Tell loved ones what you appreciate about them in a letter, email, or text. Handwritten messages work best and can become keepsakes. If you are short on time, compliment someone or simply tell them you care. Bring joy to someone else's heart. Human beings are altruistic by nature and flourish best when they lift others up.

- Take a walk alone or with a treasured pet. Take in nature and the beauty around you. Be present to notice all the good in the world.

- Meditate or just be still for ten minutes a day. There are many meditation strategies out there, but it's important to find one that you will use. Maybe you like a voice guiding you. Maybe you enjoy music, Tibetan gongs, or nature sounds. Whatever you need, just do it. You do not have to be good at meditating. Merely practicing being still and breathing

deeply will have profound effects. Pair meditation with heartfelt appreciation for the best
results.

When adopting new healthy exercises, focus on progress, not perfection. Get rid of your all-or-nothing attitude.
If you only meditate four times this week instead of seven,
do not beat yourself up. That's still a lot more than zero. If
you talk about what you're grateful for over breakfast with
your kids one day and forget to do it again for a week, so
be it. Just keep practicing. Nothing dampens our healthy
efforts more than focusing on failure.

The more you call the things you are grateful for into
awareness, the more you will see. Gratitude is about appreciation, and what you appreciate will appreciate. That's
a promise.

9. LOVE YOURSELF

"Imperfection is beauty, madness is genius and it's better to be absolutely ridiculous than absolutely boring."

– Marilyn Monroe

Growing up, I was the middle child and the only girl out of three. I never made waves like my big brother, the wild child who kept everyone on their knees and toes. Indeed, I was exceptionally reserved and quiet. When I was two, my mother took me to the doctor to make sure there was nothing wrong with me because I was "so good." As a teenager, I was often the designated driver, making sure my friends were home by curfew.

Perhaps I sensed on some level that my folks didn't have the best relationship. I also felt a sense of purpose in not creating more hardship for our parents. Whatever the reason, I found refuge in my autonomy. No one had to tell me to do my homework or do the right thing. It was expected and I delivered. Looking back, I wonder if I was protecting my family or myself.

I grew up doing everything "right." I went to church, got good grades, played sports, and had a group of friends that never got into trouble. I went to a good college, got a great job after graduation, fell in love, got married, and had kids—all in the order that society expected of me.

I never suffered from any debilitating insecurities. My personality worked for me as a student and then as a human resources manager. In all areas of life, my autonomy was an asset and an invaluable resource. Then I had my first child.

I remember looking down at the infant in my arms with his shiny mop of dark hair and thinking I'd never felt such overwhelming love ... or vulnerability.

The feeling was both foreign and frightening. I felt exposed. I needed my son, and I needed help caring for him. This combination of vulnerability and dependence would set the stage for hardship. I'd never learned how to accept either.

People like me who color within the lines, follow the rules, and never stray from the conventional path are often pretty boring. Following a predetermined path leaves little room for color or possibility. Yet the first step in self-love is not limiting yourself. So, let's explore how playing by the rules can lead us astray.

Convention tells us to get straight A's while placing little importance on curiosity or creativity. By prioritizing grades and standardized tests, the typical American education system destroys critical thinking, disengages children who learn differently, and in many cases, stifles love of learning.

Convention will convince you that intelligence can be measured by IQ, implying that it's a genetic trait. The truth is that cleverness and stupidity can both be cultivated. We expand our minds by learning and experiencing new things. We remain ignorant when we willfully reject new ideas and understanding.

Convention will tell you to follow the approved path for success and social acceptance, neglecting to mention that living authentically will liberate you.

Convention persuades us that money, status, and material things will give us a great life, without explaining that happiness is an inside job.

Convention tells us that love is automatically perfect, instead of admitting it requires work and attention.

Convention will tell you to be productive, but not that excessive busyness can rob you of presence, creativity, and joy.

Convention will tell you that you need to "find" yourself, when you may need to create the person you want to be.

Conventional thinking is exactly why so many people do not live their truth. Too many of us are living fantasies that society shoved down our throats. Then we wonder why we feel disconnected.

When I became a mother, I had to shift in ways that were new and uncomfortable. I resisted that calling because I did not understand it, nor did I know I *could* be different. Society told us our personalities are permanent, and we believed it, ignoring how uniquely equipped the human brain is for possibility and potential.

Advances in neuroscience have helped us better understand our brains, minds, and behavior. The long-held scientific belief of a fixed and compartmentalized brain was destroyed in the 1970s by Michael Merzenich, who was actually hoping to prove the old theory. Neuroplasticity is defined as "the ability of the brain to form and reorganize synaptic connections, especially in response to learning or experience or following injury."

Not only can we transform our minds, but that is the natural direction. Our brains were created for expansion, not stagnation. "Thinking, learning and acting actually change both the brain's functional anatomy from top to bottom, and its physical anatomy."[4] Unsurprisingly, a healthy mind is one that is exercised. That means challenging it with new ideas, in order to sprout new neural connections.

We are called to learn every day of our lives, yet many of us resist it. We like our limited stories because familiar discomfort is preferable to the dread of the unknown. We know that biology is a powerful regenerative force. We have the choice to assume that power or neglect it. Life is an odyssey of transformation. Nothing is truly alive once it has stopped growing.

Pay attention to negative thoughts, which are both the cause and the result of unfulfilled potential. Make no mistake, suffering has a purpose. It can be a teacher and a path to freedom. After all, we can't know darkness without light, nor joy without pain. Yet remember what I told you. We cannot anesthetize one emotion without freezing all of them. If you are permanently numb or exclusively negative, that demonstrates a lack of personal evolution.

My resistance to growth stemmed from a reluctance to appear needy or weak. I saw myself as invincible, so I rejected anything that suggested otherwise. Instead of admitting my shortcomings as a wife and mom, I doubled down on my strengths to make up for them. This is something many people do when transformation knocks. They find a way to reinforce their identity and prove to themselves that they cannot change.

I'd spent a lifetime proving my strength, only to turn around and resent a husband who could not recognize my hidden needs. When it came down to it, I manifested the dynamic where I needed help and didn't get it because I was proud of appearing autonomous. I didn't realize needing someone could be a sign of a relationship's strength, and not my personal weakness.

How do you know if you are being called upon to grow? There are several telltale signs. If you are often judgmental of others, it is usually a projection of judgment on yourself. Another indication is frequent use of excuses to justify your actions. The most visible sign is often the least obvious. Maybe you often find yourself overwhelmed with low-level emotions such as fear, anxiety, worry, anger, hate, shame, or guilt. Your emotional state is your alarm system. The siren will go off when the mind detects trouble and become louder and louder until you address it.

Self-love is not about looking in the mirror and telling yourself how wonderful you are. It means demanding more of yourself and not settling for less. Stop dieting to punish your body. Eat healthy foods that nourish and respect it instead. Believe you can become whatever you aspire to, and that you're worthy of the effort to get there. Be kinder, more forgiving, and less judgmental of yourself. It will also make you kinder, more forgiving, and less judgmental of others.

Loving yourself also means seeking your own path. Scribble furiously and colorfully outside of the lines. Speak your truth. Break the rules. Be creative and curious. Expand your mind. Learn, grow, and liberate yourself from every belief that keeps you small and scared.

10. MANIFEST WHAT YOU WANT

"Don't wait for your feelings to change to take action. Take action and your feelings will change."

– Barbara Baron

When it was time to talk seriously about divorce, we had to put it all on the table. I had to tell my husband everything, no matter how much it hurt him. I told Mario I felt like an empty shell, that my love for him was long gone and I had no idea how I was going to get it back.

Deep down, he wasn't surprised. He also knew how difficult going forward would be because of it. I was willing to do everything I could to open myself back up, but he needed to understand how far gone I was and set his expectations low for rapid improvement.

When I told him I no longer loved him, he said, "I don't want you to say you love me until you can say it honestly." I'd never been one to fake emotions or say something I didn't mean, so that worked for me. But the next day, he woke up with a different plan.

"I changed my mind. I want you to tell me you love me every single day."

I was a tad annoyed. He knew how difficult it would be for me to voice something I didn't believe, especially now that we were trying to be honest. I have never been a good actress and couldn't understand why he wanted me to pretend. I wondered if he just needed to hear it, even if it was a lie.

I could have reacted from my usual place of resentment. He was asking for more effort from me than was fair, but I resisted the urge to protest. In the end, this turned out to be a climactic move for our relationship. For the first time in ten years, I responded with empathy.

When we use words like manifesting and affirmations, people immediately think woo-woo pseudoscience. Let's break these words down into what they actually mean. To affirm something is "to state it as a fact, to assert strongly and publicly." To manifest is "to demonstrate or to make clear or obvious."

We all use affirmations every day, usually without any intention. You may not be using these pronouncements to deliberately manifest your reality. Yet when you assert the same statement day after day, what do you expect to come of your obsession? How many times a day do you assert the bad about yourself, your spouse, or your life, whether verbally or inside your head? I declared my grudge toward my husband every day for ten years. I recited in my head every day that I did not like him, and I got exactly what I affirmed. I manifested a miserable relationship instead of a beautiful one.

I think words like affirmation and manifestation are used by the spiritual because they understand how powerful thoughts and words are to our experience. It helps if you are more attuned to what you are feeling on the inside, as opposed to the external. Most of us go through life never observing our thoughts or trying to understand how they master our existence. Our actions are guided by habits rather than intention and possibility. These patterns become what we call the self. We continuously enforce that identity, then use it to justify why we never change or reach our potential.

We all need to understand how thoughts can influence

our physical being. We need to understand the difference between belief, opinion, and fact. We have to observe how our minds and emotions rule our lives. Only then can we evolve into human beings who affirm what they want, instead of what they don't want.

When Mario wanted me to tell him I loved him every day, he was asking me to love deliberately. Rather than sit back and wait for the feelings to return, he wanted me to prove it to him, and to myself, through my words and actions.

More important than the words themselves was the act of making myself declare them. I had to break down the walls I'd stubbornly maintained to give my husband verbal confirmation that I *wanted* to love him. This was something the old, angry Cindy never would have done. Maybe on some level, Mario knew that. This was a softening on my part, and arguably my first real act of love in years. As soon as I gave Mario what he needed, my anger began to dissolve. Once I let those walls crumble, I could expose and open my heart again.

I did not realize it at the time but giving in to my husband opened my heart up to receive my own needs. Throughout my life, I'd never allowed myself to need anyone, even my husband. I also resented any instance where he, or anybody, needed me beyond my expectations. There was no back-and-forth flow of giving and receiving anywhere in my life. It felt like everyone just took from me. Opening up the channels to both give and take was a powerful shift.

To change your situation, start with your response. Let go of the emotions keeping you from choosing love. If you are as far gone as I was, you may be telling yourself that you do not want to love your partner again. Instead, ask yourself if you want to keep hating him. No one wants to be consumed with negativity. That stuff spews from your pores and coats everyone and everything around you. It's poison to your soul.

I know you want love and connection, because we all do. If your spouse is worth it, start to affirm the relationship you want. Let go of the part of you that got you into this mess. Isn't that ultimately what you want? To not think or feel this way anymore?

I know this is a lot to wrap your head around. I could not see all of this when I was in the thick of it. You have to walk before you can run. At first, I just focused on monitoring my thoughts and emotional state. Eventually I was able to stop concentrating on what I disliked and manifest more of what I liked about my marriage. Every day, I made deliberate decisions that reflected what I wanted for myself and my family. Over time, my intentions became reality.

11. THINK ABOUT YOUR THINKING

"What is necessary to change any person
is to change his awareness of himself."

– Abraham Maslow

In order to think clearly and make good decisions, I had to shift away from the stress and pain that had overwhelmed me since the birth of my second child. It was more than just my husband. My parents were going through a nasty divorce and I found myself caught between them. As their on-call counselor, I was learning more about their personal lives than any child should know about their mom and dad. They went from being married one day to being unable to stay in the same room the next. This, after three kids, two grandkids, and thirty-seven years of marriage. It made no sense and broke my heart in ways I still cannot explain.

To top off the trifecta, we were also doing a massive renovation and new construction on our house. Just a few years after that huge effort, we moved across the country from Boston to Texas, because Mario wanted to pursue other opportunities. Had he asked me to move before my parents got divorced, I would have said no. Yet the idea of escaping the discomfort and sadness I now felt at every holiday and family gathering was suddenly very appealing, so I agreed. Five months later, we packed all of our belongings in the middle of a Boston ice storm and flew to Texas. Maybe part of me thought a new beginning would help my own marriage, too. I'll be honest, though—I wasn't thinking much at all. I was just trying to survive.

I had all of this going on, and no idea how to handle it, so I let it handle me instead. Not once did I consider that I could exert control over my thoughts or emotions. I knew I was responsible for my actions, but I never understood how they manifested first as thoughts.

Why do some people react calmly to getting cut off in traffic, while others scream obscenities and bring their car right up to the offending bumper threateningly? How can one parent sit peacefully on the sidelines of their kid's soccer game, while another is driven to scream and yell at the referee? How can one person accomplish all their goals, while others struggle to get out of their own way? How does one person thrive after a traumatic childhood, while another becomes a drug addict? How does one person lose fifty pounds and keep it off forever, while many more cycle endlessly through fad diets?

Why do we act the way we do, and how do we change our unwanted behavior? What is the genesis of human behavior? I found the answers when I discovered two books about neuroscience. The first was called *You Are the Placebo*, by Dr. Joe Dispenza. The other was called *Buddha's Brain*, by Rick Hanson, Ph.D., and Richard Mendius, M.D.

These books taught me how to focus less on behavior and more on the thoughts in my head. I learned that we have upwards of 100 billion neurons in our brains that transmit electrochemical messages to one another. Think of your brain as a tree with many branches that shuttle information from neuron to neuron. Every time you learn something new, your tree grows as a connecting branch is formed in the brain. When the experience is replicated over and over again, those neural connections become stronger, and that "branch" in your neural network gets thicker.

Those thicker branches eventually become habits that can be difficult to break. Habits don't apply only to behavior; they start as repeated patterns of thought. These repeated subconscious thoughts then create related emotional and behavioral patterns. All habits become increasingly ingrained until they can be performed with hardly any consciousness at all.

A great example of how learning becomes mindless is driving. When a teenager first learns how to drive, their neural networks are actively sprouting new connections. At first, they have to think about everything: how to put the car in reverse, how to turn the steering wheel, how much pressure to put on the gas pedal, and when to use the blinker. They have to walk themselves through the process. Their brains aren't doing it automatically.

Now think about the last time you drove a car. You likely don't recall putting the car in reverse, parking, or even going from Point A to Point B. The neural connections that fire off when we drive have gotten so strong that it has become automatic. Habits are formed by repetitive actions, which are initiated by thoughts. Before driving became routine, we had to condition our minds by using our "thinking brain" to learn how. Once we could execute the task effortlessly, more primitive parts of the brain took over.

Understanding my brain and how behavior began was crucial to helping me change my mind. I strongly believe we need to understand how our misery becomes an emotional habit. Only then do we have the power to take back control. Unfortunately, bad habits are often created easily and unconsciously. Forming good ones, on the other hand, requires effort and purpose. That is why bad habits often persist when good ones are not created to combat them. Most people lack the awareness to form better habits. They are asleep at the wheel, wondering why they have no agency. We feel powerless when we don't fully utilize the most evolved part of ourselves, the "thinking" brain. In *How to Change Your Mind*, Michael Pollan writes,

> One's self—this ever-present voice in the head, this ceaselessly commenting, interpreting, labeling, defending I—becomes perhaps a little too familiar. I'm not talking about anything as deep as self-knowledge here. No, just about how, over time, we tend to optimize and conventionalize our responses to whatever life brings. Each of us develops our shorthand ways of slotting and processing everyday experiences and solving problems, and while this is no doubt adaptive—it helps us get the job done with minimum of fuss—eventually it becomes rote. It dulls us. The muscles of attention atrophy. Habits are undeniably useful tools, reliev-

ing us of the need to run a complex mental operation every time we're confronted with a new task or situation. Yet they also relieve us of the need to stay awake to the world: to attend, feel, think, and then act in a deliberate manner. (That is, from freedom rather than compulsion.)

Neuroscientists use a term called "metacognition" to denote a concept most people never consider. It's defined as "thinking about your thinking."

We have a thought (usually unconsciously). That thought creates an emotion, which leads to a behavior. This pattern repeats with the same thought, day in and day out. It is said that we have hundreds of thousands of thoughts each day, and the vast majority of those thoughts are repeated over and over. That means we are both boring and completely comatose to the power we have to change our lives.

Understanding these basic ideas from a scientific perspective gave me the knowledge I needed to understand how human beings transform. More importantly, this information changed what I thought was possible. I was no longer a slave to my unwanted compulsions. I had the freedom to choose differently.

I knew changing my life had to start in my mind, so I

began practicing metacognition. I was more aware of what I felt than what I was thinking, so I let my emotions be my guide. They became the trigger in my strategy. Any thought or belief that produced an unpleasant feeling was a thought or belief that I had to explore and revise. As soon as I felt a negative emotion, I would stop and think about my thinking. I'd ask, "What would I have to believe in order to feel more positive right now?" If that didn't work, I practiced gratitude.

On the journey back to my husband, I had many emotional triggers. The patterns I had cultivated for ten years did not disappear overnight. I was still frustrated and annoyed, but my newfound knowledge made these emotions less potent. My life still felt like a prison, but this understanding gave me an escape plan.

Understanding how the mind works allowed me to boot up a brand-new operating system on my brain. I learned to define adverse reactions differently and embrace them as part of my process. Discomfort was a necessary by-product of transformation. I had to see my pain less as something to be avoided and more as a lifeline to experiencing joy. It had to be uncomfortable, disruptive, and inconvenient. If it wasn't, then I wasn't changing.

It is vital to your mental renovation that you pay attention to what you are thinking and feeling. In an unhappy marriage, you likely spend a lot of time thinking about everything you dislike about your spouse. If you choose to focus on those things, you will always find what you are looking for and will miss all the good that sits outside your focus.

If I asked you to drive for two miles and count all the white cars you saw, you would be able to give me a fairly accurate sum. If I then asked you to tell me how many red cars were along that route, you likely wouldn't be as sure. You were so focused on counting the white cars that you neglected to see the red ones.

I'd trained the spotlight on what Mario did wrong and couldn't see what he was doing right. Realizing this, I started thinking more about the things I loved about our life together. I thought back on what made me fall in love with my husband in the first place, tapping into memories that were rich with love and friendship. When I did that, I realized my husband still had many of the same qualities he'd had before. The more I focused on my husband's good traits, the more I found. The negative memories were soon crowded out, just like the red cars.

> *"When you change the way you look at things, the things you look at change."*
>
> – Wayne Dyer

12. ENGAGE

*"The secret of change is to focus all of
your energy, not on fighting the old, but
on building the new."*

– Dan Millman

This quote encapsulates the secret of transformation. Write it down on a sticky note and put it on your mirror to remind yourself every day.

As you know by now, "How do I stop hating my husband?" was the wrong question. You cannot engage in the act of *not* doing something. What happens when you try to "not think" about someone? You think about them.

When my college sweetheart broke my heart, I huddled in fetal position on my bed bawling my eyes to "Against

All Odds" by Phil Collins on repeat. Wallowing in sappy love songs did nothing to help me get over my former love. What did help? Finally replacing my old relationship with a new one. Not so fast, girl! You don't have to replace your husband. Just start a new relationship with him.

Mario and I did this by coming up with a game plan. Before you scoff, let me tell you this simple exercise helped when expensive couple's therapy didn't. We went to sessions every week for months with little progress. In every appointment, we rehashed our past. I'd cry and remember how miserable I was all those years, then nothing would change.

One day, after a particularly wretched counseling session, Mario and I sat down at home to talk by ourselves. We knew how we'd gotten to this place. We had already decided to forgive each other and form a new relationship to replace the old, broken one. We both felt that therapy was holding us back because it forced us to keep revisiting old emotions and behavior patterns. Every week we reverted to our old selves. Yet we would never move forward if we stayed in the past.

We were beyond the point of blaming each other. Each of us took responsibility for the role we played. We knew we could not change each other. We also knew that a transformed relationship required transformed people, so we had to focus on changing ourselves.

We were sick of living in the past and decided we had to build something new. Working together, we mapped out our romance business plan, starting with a list of what a happy and healthy marriage looked like to each of us.

We agreed that in a healthy union, couples communicated well and often. Going forward, we would be open about how we felt and allow ourselves to be vulnerable. We would clarify situations with each other instead of making assumptions or fabricating our own explanations. If something made us sad or insecure, we would give the other person the benefit of the doubt and ask for their side of the story. To facilitate this, we would use the following format:

"When you said _____ or did _____, it made me think or feel _____. Can you tell me what you meant to convey, if anything, with your words or behaviors?"

We also made an effort to reach out to each other more during the day when we were apart. It did not have to be an ongoing conversation. The point was to show effort. A simple "Hi, thinking of you" text went a long way.

Happy couples also know their love languages. If you haven't taken the Love Language test, I highly recommend it (you can find it online at https://www.5lovelanguages.

com/quizzes/). This will help you understand where you went wrong displaying your love to one another.

My love language was the most unromantic of the five: Acts of Service. I felt loved when people did things for me. I also showed affection by doing things for the people I loved.

My husband's love language was Quality Time, which explained a lot. I felt unloved because Mario never helped me with my to-do list. Mario felt unwanted because I never spent time with him. Once we discovered our love languages, we realized that if he helped me with chores, I would have more time to spend with him. This was a game changer for our marriage. Having the same love language is not necessary for a couple. The reason for taking the test is to discover how we all express love differently.

Another thing happy couples do is flirt. They have date nights, hold hands, and sit close to each other on the couch. My job was learning to be more playful. It wasn't just about being flirty, but also more fun. I wanted my kids to see us enjoying each other instead of feeling a cold draft between us. Have you ever seen the look on your child's face when you hug or kiss your spouse in front of them? It's pure magic.

To work toward this objective, we made sure to go on dates once a week. We'd always shared a love for food and films. These date nights brought back memories of when we first got together. Before we had kids, we often frequented the movie theater. We always left before the credits rolled to avoid the crowds. To this day, he still makes a run for it. Now I like to take my time but seeing him take off before the lights go on still makes me smile. Entertaining in our home and spending time with friends and loved ones was also affirming to our relationship, because it reminded us of what we'd built and still shared as a couple.

Physical affection is another great way to feel close. Mario and I started holding hands when we were out, even if it was just for a few minutes while driving or walking down the street. We made sure to sit more closely on the couch, usually with our adorable cockapoos draped over our laps. (Nothing brings a couple closer than cockapoos.) We weren't trying to be attached at the hip, but simply making an effort to touch.

Strong couples refer to themselves as "we." Once we became parents, it seemed we operated more like a business than a pair. Mario had his role and I had mine. Our jobs rarely crossed paths. He was the breadwinner who spent most of the day at work. I was the homemaker and full-time mom. Being a team required us to give, receive, and need. I knew how to give, but I never allowed myself to do the latter two. To feel more connected, we had to blur the boundaries of our roles so that we could feel less separate.

If my sons, Alex and Andrew, Dad or my brothers are reading this, FULL STOP NOW. Sex talk ahead. Please skip the next couple of paragraphs. Trust me, you do not want to read this part. I will cue you in bold when it is okay to come back.

Great couples have sex often, so Mario and I made it a goal to have sex at least two to three times a week. At the time, this was my least favorite part of our relationship plan, but I understood it was crucial for our recovery.

Sex is such a fundamental part of a strong marriage. If you and your spouse have never had a good sex life, it may be worth seeing a specialized therapist. If you once had a good sex life and want to get it back, start by allowing yourself to open up again. If your spouse has to chase away penguins every time he gets in bed with you, it's on you to become warm again. Do whatever it takes to get out of your head and into your groove. Maybe that's tequila, *Fifty Shades of Grey*, or a few episodes of the first season of *Outlander*. Be willing to try things that help get you in the mood. The walls must come down to have mutually enjoyable sex, and practice helps.

Alex, Andrew, Dad and brothers, you can continue reading from here...

A happy marriage also includes spending time as a family. For me, this meant reconnecting with mine after a decade of disengagement. We did that by cooking together, eating meals at the dinner table, doing puzzles, playing games, going to movies, and taking vacations as a family. It's important to prioritize time for bonding. As human beings, we all desire a sense of belonging. Yet many families are too busy to spend time together, whether because both parents work full time or because they're so busy with other activities that they're never home. Busyness robs us of memories and the things that matter. Strengthening ties through quality time together is good for your health, your marriage, and your family.

Healthy couples invest in their home. This isn't about money but about sharing a mutual refuge. When we are unhappy, we often disconnect from things we have in common. I invested the bare minimum of time and effort in our house when I detached emotionally. One of the first things I did in recovery was redesign the living room by making everything white. I wanted to walk into this clean new room every morning and spread my love over it like peanut butter. With a few coats of paint, this room became symbolic of my effort to appreciate and love my life again. Since then, I have created a garden in my yard, hanging feeders, birdbaths, birdhouses, wind chimes, and more. Now home really is where my heart is.

Lastly, loving couples have separate interests. At the beginning, this was my favorite part of our relationship plan and the easiest for us to achieve. We knew that spending every waking moment together did not indicate a healthy relationship. It's important to have shared interests, but we also had to maintain our individuality to remain well-rounded and interesting to one another.

Those were the healthy and happy couple goals that we created together. Notice that not once did I mention what happy and healthy couples *don't* do. Again, that's because targeting what not to do will take the spotlight off the things you should be doing more.

We get more of what we engage in. Most people at the end of their ropes detach from their relationships, family, and home. They wonder why they feel so disconnected, never stopping to consider that love and engagement could be actions rather than feelings. Healthy and happy marriages, like healthy and happy people, do not come about through luck. They must be cultivated through action. Plan the relationship you want and engage in the activities that will bring you and your spouse closer together.

13. RESET YOUR MINDSET

"Why waste time proving over and over how great you are, when you could be getting better? Why hide deficiencies instead of overcoming them? Why look for friends or partners who will just shore up your self-esteem instead of ones who will also challenge you to grow? And why seek out the tried and true, instead of experiences that will stretch you? The passion for stretching yourself and sticking to it, even (or especially) when it's not going well, is the hallmark of the growth mindset. This is the mindset that

*allows people to thrive during some of
the most challenging times in their lives."*

– Carol S. Dweck

Many people categorize themselves or others as having a positive or negative "mindset" but cannot adequately explain what that is, or how a positive or negative outlook is created. In psychology, a mindset is a set of beliefs that determine the way you act and respond to situations.

Our mentality is governed by beliefs that are often formed in childhood, typically as a result of influential adults like parents, teachers, coaches, or clergymen. These beliefs can stay with us permanently or evolve as we grow and challenge them.

We don't see the world as it is, we see the world as we are. Someone with a mindset oriented around learning will be adaptable and open to growth. Someone with a fixed mindset, who believes that people are incapable of change, will generally stay the same. It is really that simple.

Beliefs can shift when we experience something that refutes them, or when we deliberately challenge them. They crumble when we realize our views are not based on fact but on our own limited experience. Someone with a fixed mindset will therefore minimize their exposure to new ideas and knowledge that might contradict their beliefs.

Researcher Carol Dweck, Ph.D., author of the groundbreaking book *Mindset*, discovered that people with fixed mindsets are more apt to lie, cheat, blame, justify, and become depressed. These people believe traits like intelligence are innate rather than the result of learning new things. In their minds, there is nothing you can do to become smarter. You are who you are. This belief then becomes a self-fulfilling prophecy.

They may reject education because they fear failure—or worse, being discovered for their shameful secret. There is a powerful cognitive difference between a person who thinks their attributes are immutable and one who believes they can change through training and effort. One creates a life of shame, fear, and powerlessness, while the other fosters a life of empowerment, curiosity, and growth.

We have all heard the phrase "limiting beliefs," or ideas we tell ourselves that keep us feeling small. Yet we cannot just "get over" our limiting beliefs without a much deeper understanding of mindset and how it alters our perception.

Our beliefs shape our reality. They dictate what we look for, focus on, and therefore what we experience. They are also unique to what we have lived through, which is why one person's opinions can differ drastically from the next. In forty-three years of life, I never thought about my thinking or questioned what I believed.

When I began to look inside, I wondered how many of my beliefs were learned from someone I'd trusted or ideas I'd settled on, rather than something I'd actually experienced. I knew I was organized, which was a good thing, and a skill I continued to cultivate. I wasn't usually creative, so I never took part in creative activities. We all think of ourselves in terms of what we are and aren't. We settle on who we are far too easily, and those ideas go undisputed. How many of your closely held beliefs have you questioned? Do you want to be the person you have defined? Are there new traits you would like to cultivate within yourself?

These questions are important to explore. Everything in your life comes down to how you think. The set of beliefs that govern your personality will also dictate what you assume about others and the world. When you look for confirmation of those ideas, chances are that's what you'll find. Limiting your mind will restrict your life. Opening it up allows for expansion.

This is why it's so difficult for people to transform their bodies, relationships, or circumstances. They rely on willpower and brute force to alter behavior, when the problem was created by their minds. To change how you act, you must first change how you think.

Dweck describes two types of attitudes in her book. The first is a fixed mindset which believes that human qualities like skills, intelligence, and personality are fixed at birth. We are born athletic or smart or "type A." If you have "two left feet" as a child, you can forget about joining the Royal Ballet. If you score low on an IQ test, then you'll never be smart.

We all demonstrate some level of immobility. Any part of our personality we believe can't be changed is the product of a fixed mindset. It is important to recognize when we do this and whether or not this attitude holds us back from something we want. For instance, I know I can't sing. Could I sound okay with the right training or voice coach? Maybe, but that's not something I desire for myself. Nor has my lack of talent ever stopped me from singing "Don't Stop Believin'" at the top of my lungs in a solo rendition of Carpool Karaoke.

People with completely fixed minds are a different story. They perceive the self as unalterable, which engenders a sense of powerlessness. You are born the way you are. If you don't like it, too bad. Fixed thinkers often turn to illicit behavior to cover up for their perceived deficiencies. Accountability only matters if you intend to learn from your mistakes. People with fixed mindsets do not understand this concept. For them, improvement is not an option.

We see the world as we see ourselves. If we believe human characteristics to be immutable, we are often more judgmental. This is because we are covering up our own insecurities by diverting criticism elsewhere. People with fixed mindsets are more apt to use stereotypes and labels, which signifies belonging (and hiding) within a group. Labels also allow us to judge without ever getting to know someone, often ignoring character or actual behavior.

The character of Javert in the *Les Miserables* movie epitomizes the fixed mindset. Javert, a law-and-order policeman, saw Jean Valjean as a criminal. It did not matter that Valjean only stole a loaf of bread to feed his starving family, or that he had served time as a slave as punishment. In Javert's mind, anyone who broke the rules was a bad man, no matter the circumstances.

Throughout the movie, Jean Valjean proves over and over again to be a man of virtue and empathy. Yet he cannot redeem himself. Javert continues to see Valjean as a bad man because of his criminal record. I recommend watching the movie and paying close attention to this idea. Take note of the end when Javert experiences something so powerful that it finally fractures his fixed beliefs. The end demonstrates how our beliefs can create an identity so rigid and inflexible that if or when it shatters, it destroys our entire worldview and thus how we see ourselves in the world.

Fixed thinkers deem others to be what they imagine about themselves. Someone who believes their intelligence is predetermined may cheat because they don't think they can learn. Cheating, therefore, is the only way to succeed and they feel justified doing it. They may also lie to hide self-perceived defects rather than ask for help. They often feel no agency over their life and exert what control they can through other means.

Growth-minded folks believe we can cultivate all the traits that fixed mindsets believe are locked at birth. They tend to focus more on individuality than on broad categorization. They are less insecure because they view flaws as opportunities for growth. They are typically more curious, more accountable, and less anxious. As Dweck points out, the primary difference between the two belief systems manifests as "being" the way you are forever versus "becoming" anything that you desire.

A fixed mind is hard, closed, and permanent like a brick wall. It ignores the neuroplasticity of our brains and their ability to grow, adapt, or learn. A growth mindset takes advantage of our mind's natural state and its ability to reorganize. Too many of us are denying our mind's natural flexibility, plasticity, and potential because of our beliefs. Our minds are biologically designed for expansion, but not everyone has the right mindset to seize it.

The older people are, the harder a fixed mindset is to break. Their identities and dogmas have had years to solidify. Yet, I am optimistic because we have seen trees grow through concrete and rivers flow through rock. The flow of our nature will take over if we let it.

Many of us have a certain degree of both the fixed and the growth mindset. I had a fixed mindset about my creativity. I identified as "Type A" so I believed that I "didn't have a creative bone in my body." I've said this about myself throughout my entire life. (I affirmed it.) In reality, my complete focus on my Type-A skill set crowded out any possibility for creative thinking.

In my mind, originality was also limited to the arts. Since I could not draw, sing, dance, or play a musical instrument, I labeled myself as "not creative." In fact, I was limiting the scope of creativity. I did not realize that imagination could be expressed through playing, growing, or simply coming up with ideas. By lasering in on my Type-A tendencies, I became imbalanced. I rarely stopped to appreciate art or nature, both of which seemed like distractions from my productivity. Far from engaging in my creative side, I doubled down on efficiency to make up for what I viewed as a shortcoming imagination-wise.

Liberation comes through creativity, and we all have the potential for it. We can tap into our creative side by slowing down and appreciating all that is beautiful. I threw out my limited definition of creativity and focused on this one instead:

"Creativity is inventing, experimenting, growing, taking risks, breaking rules, making mistakes, and having fun."

– Mary Lou Cook

It takes no special skills to invent, experiment, grow, take risks, break rules, make mistakes, or have fun. Yet as a perfectionist, I once had little tolerance for fun or patience for drawing outside the lines.

When I decided to transform my marriage, I was choosing to change how I engaged with it. It also meant changing how I engaged with life. How you do one thing is how you do everything. I took parts of my personality that weren't serving me and cultivated a different side.

My Type-A personality was useful for getting things done, but it also made me inflexible. It stole my joy and robbed me of the ability to be present. Having people over for dinner, I was more concerned with the work it entailed than the closeness and connection it would yield. When I stopped to think about it, I wanted people to feel comfortable in my home. I didn't want to be the person who whipped out the vacuum cleaner the second guests left. My sister-in-law recalled a time before I had kids when her family came over for dinner and I actually took the vacuum out *before* they left.

I also wanted to slow down and exude a less rigid energy. I hated feeling frustrated and impatient all the time. It wasn't until I set out to reinvent my marriage that I learned I could cultivate a more playful personality. If you had told me fifteen years ago that I could be creative and flexible, I would have said, "No I can't, it's just not me."

I had a fixed mindset for many, many years. Our identities can hold us back when they are rooted in old ideas. My personality served me well for a long time—until it didn't. I stopped evolving, which played a role in how I (mis)handled challenges in my marriage.

I want to share another personal fixed mindset story unrelated to my marriage or personality, because I'm sure some of you can relate. I always loved running. I was a distance runner from the time I was fourteen years old. In my twenties, I ran the New York City Marathon three times. My best time was four hours and ten minutes.

My dream marathon, however, was not only the oldest and most prestigious, it was in my hometown. I'd watch the Boston Marathon and fantasize about crossing the finish line, but I never dreamed I could qualify.

When I worked in Boston, I remember smoldering with envy when a coworker who picked up running later in life managed to secure one of the coveted spots. There was an option to raise money and run for a charity, but that wasn't good enough. I didn't want to run Boston *just* to run Boston. I wanted to run as one of the elites that qualified.

For ten years, I watched other runners achieve my dream. I told myself that I wasn't fast enough. I didn't believe I was worthy. But the race remained in the back of my mind. It haunted me every year as I played the familiar role of spectator.

I had a fixed mindset about my running ability. I'd run the New York Marathon three times with no issues whatsoever, but my best time was still twenty-five minutes too long to qualify for Boston. Every time I ran the New York Marathon, I trained to finish, not to win. I believed that I did not have the speed to qualify, and this belief alone kept me from trying.

After my second child was born, I ran a 10K with a friend. This race was a "there-and-back," which meant you ran from Point A to Point B and then back to Point A, creating an overlap. As you're running toward Point B, the people ahead of you are running toward you on their way back to Point A, so you can see exactly who is ahead of you.

I don't recall much about the woman who inspired me that day. All I know is that she and I came nearly face to face as I was running out and she was already coming back. I remember thinking, "Geez, she's fast. She doesn't even look like she would be. If she can run that fast, surely I can."

During that race, I pushed myself to run faster, all because this unknown woman, who didn't look like she was built for speed, was beating me. For years, I'd harbored some unconscious stereotype about what a "fast runner" looked like, and neither she nor I fit that mold. This woman decimated that belief, and I finished that race faster than I ever thought I could. As I crossed the finish line, I thought "Huh, maybe I *am* fast enough for the Boston Marathon..."

It wasn't until I learned about limiting beliefs that I understood what happened that day. My brief encounter with that woman made me rethink a long-held belief, not only about myself but about fast runners in general. Many people in that situation might double down on their belief and reject what they were experiencing. That's because when an important belief is challenged, what it's really doing is challenging our identity.

I had an open mind that allowed for growth. Instead of saying, "Nope, I am not fast enough," I accepted the new paradigm, which enabled me to speed up instantly. I finished the race faster than I'd ever run in my adult life, and my limiting belief was shattered. That idea was a new door, and I sprinted through it.

A moment of reckoning was all it took for me to finally go after a dream I'd harbored for years. After that race, I took a different approach and dove into research on running faster. I signed up for a qualifying marathon and began a new training plan designed for speed.

This new regimen was nothing like the training I did to run the NYC marathons. I did speed workouts twice a week, one at a track and one just running eight miles as fast as I could. By the time the race came around, I was clocking in under-nine-minute miles on my long runs.

When the big day came, it was brisk and windy after a rainstorm the night before. The roads were slick with wet fall leaves and muddy puddles. I knew I would have to push myself to my limit for the entire 26.2 miles.

I remember only two points in the race. The first was at the twenty-mile mark, when I felt like I could not make it at my pace for another six miles. I just wanted it to be over. The second was coming toward the finish line. I ran onto the final stretch of track with maybe two hundred meters left to go. I remember the feeling of gravel under my feet, the crunchy noise my shoes made on the dirt, and my heavy breathing. I felt like I was running in slow motion.

As I rounded the corner and saw the finish line clock, I could not believe my eyes. I fought back tears, so overwhelmed with joy and pain that it took my breath away.

The clock read three hours and twenty-one minutes as I crossed the finish line. I not only made my qualifying time, I conquered it by twenty-four minutes. For ten years, I'd wanted to run the Boston Marathon but didn't try to qualify because I didn't think I was fast enough. I set my mind to believe that I could not do it, so I never did.

When we limit our beliefs, we limit our potential. That is what I came to understand after that experience. Our desires to become more, and do more, know us better than we do. Our higher self is constantly jumping up and down trying to get our attention, and too many of us let our insecurities zap her power to inspire us.

My journey back to my husband was a lot like my path to running the Boston Marathon. I had to change my mind about what I believed was possible. I had to trade in my fixed mindset about myself, my husband, and my marriage for a growth one. I had to train and relate to my goals in a different way in order to achieve a different result.

Fixed Mindset	Growth Mindset
• Bitter and vengeful when hurt • Has a hard time forgiving • Believes people are a finished product • Seeks people, objects, and trophies to validate their worth • Believes relationships should be easy and never change • Responds with blame and by getting defensive • Has a limited set of choices • Prone to judging, demeaning, and lashing out • All about "ME"	• When hurt, tries to understand • Forgives easily • Believes people are capable of change • Seeks people who will challenge them • Believes relationships can change and grow, but it requires hard work • Needs to communicate their needs • Learns from others • Takes responsibility • Sees lots of ways to fix problems • Supports, respects, and understands others • Focused on "WE"

14. THE NEW

March 2013 was the turning point of my marriage. Had I written this memoir within a year or two of that time, the book would be very different. For one thing, it would be far more pessimistic and irrational. I could not have written this with any coherence or clarity back then.

I did not chronicle all the gritty details of our worst days because we chose, as a couple, to leave that darkness behind us. Had we held on to those memories, we could not start fresh. We never denied our experiences. We did, however, choose to forgive them and each other, because deep down we believed in each other's goodness.

We would never have understood the power of our light had we not confronted the choices that led to our darkness. We both had to take responsibility for the destruction of our marriage. Although I brought our relationship to its breaking point, my husband recognized that our marriage did not fall apart without his contribution.

I have to give Mario credit for how he reacted and engaged with me at my worst. Had he not handled me with firm grace, boundaries, and a willingness to listen, our marriage may have crumbled long before. Neither of us had a book like this, let alone a clue what we were doing. Only with hindsight could we start to piece everything together.

Somehow this man rose above his pain and did what we needed. I'm convinced that most men would have run away or retaliated against a wife who admitted she no longer loved him. Imagine telling your spouse of ten years that his touch makes you cringe and that you find yourself attracted to other men. Now imagine that your husband takes that information and dotes on you, tells you that you are beautiful, that he loves you, and that you are worth fighting for.

Both my husband and I were lucky that he did not act on his fears, pain, and insecurities. He chose instead to react from a place of hope, love, and courage. Occasionally, he used humor to help us through some of our most difficult moments. We often found ourselves joking and laughing about very serious and painful things. It was weird, but it worked for us.

Mario's courage and willingness to be vulnerable fundamentally reshaped our relationship. I cannot emphasize this enough. Hope, love, intimacy, humor, openness, and courage are contagious. They are the ultimate human desires. No one enjoys fear or pain, yet many of us act out in both, thus creating more of it in our lives.

While I give my husband the credit for setting a new paradigm in our relationship, I had to do my part to make it work. My experience with divorced parents and friends who have split up played a role, as did a willingness to hold myself accountable and believe differently.

From my point of view, divorce represented utter devastation to all involved. I'd watched my parents' thirty-seven-year marriage crumble at the same exact time that my own marital problems began. My mom and dad were married at nineteen and twenty-three, respectively, and my brother was born a year later. They started out so young. Their marriage was never ideal, or easy. They had to grow up themselves while raising us. My dad took college classes at night, and my mom held multiple jobs she could do from home. I was proud of them for making it work for nearly four decades. I also knew that my aunt and grandmother played a major supporting role.

Their eventual split was unexpected and upsetting. These feelings were front and center when it came to deliberating over my own divorce. I wanted my children to have parents that were happy and together. The pain of my parents' divorce helped saved me from my own.

I also had a friend who was trapped in her own unhappy marriage. We had taken many long walks commiserating. Both our marriages blew up around the same time. When I saw what was happening to her family, I woke up to the shitstorm brewing in my own home. It was like a mirror being held up to my face. I loved them both and saw so much worth fighting for. I believed she would regret leaving one day, so I tried to give her husband advice on saving the marriage. My actions and her perceived betrayal led to a falling out between us. With the perspective of time, I realized that everything I thought about her situation was a projection of my own. I thought she needed saving because I needed saving myself.

One of the most important choices I made was to quit identifying with my pain. Think of your discomfort like a location on your GPS. When you are pinged into the pain, it looms large and everything around it is magnified. I had to zoom out from my pain in order to see the bigger picture. The experience of my friend's separation gave me the objective lens through which to see my own situation.

Held back by pain, fixed mindsets, and limiting beliefs, that objectivity can be impossible.

I say throughout this story that I chose reason over emotion, but what really helped was choosing to observe my emotions without judgment. For too long, I'd let toxicity define me. Now I was mindful of its power. I came to understand that it was separate from me and could therefore be removed. As soon as I stopped identifying with the negativity, I was able to start eliminating it from my body, mind, and life.

I also chose to learn instead of leave. I spent a long time working on myself, mainly by reading books about neuroscience, habits, emotions, and behavior change. I studied mindset and belief systems. I filled my head with knowledge and tools that expanded my understanding of myself and helped me become the person I wanted to be.

I eventually grew out of the person I was from 2003 to 2013. I said goodbye to my old identity, instead of waving farewell to my marriage and family. I left the old Cindy in the past and gave myself the gift of a different present and future.

In the process, I have experienced both triumph and transformation. The biggest difference in my family is the laughter that now fills our home. The biggest difference in me is my newfound creativity, silliness, and insatiable love of growth. My sixteen-year-old rolls his eyes at my horrible dancing and calls me his "crazy mom" at least once a day. My hope is that he will remember me as goofy and playful when he recalls his childhood, not as the rigid perfectionist I once was.

The biggest difference in my marriage is the warm feeling of contentment and completion that now exists between Mario and me. The void inside of me is finally filled, not because my marriage is so different now, but because *I* am.

EPILOGUE

I am writing this story more than five years into a completely different relationship. I've had lots of time to grow and think about the lessons I've learned.

I realize there are people out there who should get divorced. They aren't meant to be together and splitting up would be better for all involved. Yet I also know there are people who regret divorce, and even more who suffer through marriages filled with resentment and anger rather than love and laughter. My hope is that this book will offer practical guidance to couples who know they want to make it work.

You are not alone. Marital problems are universal, as are fixed mindsets and limiting beliefs. Learning how to transform is something we can all benefit from. Fixing my marriage required the same blueprint I needed to transform myself. The best prescription I can give is to approach your thoughts, emotions, and behaviors objectively. Seek self-awareness. Use your thinking brain. Get curious. Be open to new ideas and possibilities. No matter what your marital story is, you cannot change anything without changing yourself. You are the author of your life. The power to rewrite your life story with a happier ending is in your hands.

We don't find ourselves in unhappy circumstances because of deliberate choices. On the contrary, we often end up in situations we never planned for as a result of living recklessly, without intention.

This story is about choosing and creating the life and marriage that you desire. Even if your marriage is not worth saving, these ideas can still save you—but only if you are willing to commit to your evolution and let go of your stories, excuses, and limiting beliefs. What you do next will be determined by one simple thing: what you choose to believe.

"Whether you think you can, or you think you can't, you're right."

– Henry Ford

ENDNOTES

1. https://www.sciencedaily.com/releases/2017/09/170918111833.htm
2. https://guilfordjournals.com/doi/pdf/10.1521/pdps.2017.45.4.499
3. https://neuro.hms.harvard.edu/harvard-mahoney-neuroscience-institute/brain-newsletter/and-brain-series/love-and-brain
4. https://www.edubloxtutor.com/neuroplasticity/

Made in the USA
Las Vegas, NV
27 December 2024

15437059R00090